A Sailor's Yarns
and Observations

By the same author

ISLANDS OF EXPERIENCE

A POET'S SKETCH
OF HIS BIOGRAPHY

KID ON THE RIVER

ONE LIFE'S THREAD

THE HIGHLINE TRAIL

THE COPPER SANDS

THE N.P.M.W.A.R.A.

TWO CATS FOR PUERTO RICO

A Sailor's Yarns and Observations

Dean Nichols

Resource *Publications*
An imprint of *Wipf and Stock Publishers*
199 West 8th Avenue • Eugene OR 97401

Resource Publications
A division of Wipf and Stock Publishers
199 W 8th Ave, Suite 3
Eugene, OR 97401

A Sailor's Yarns and Observations
By Nichols, Dean
Copyright©1994 by Nichols, Dean
ISBN: 1-59752-278-3
Publication date 6/27/2005
Previously published by Binford & Mort Publishing, 1994

To Ramona

Open rebuke is better
> than secret love.
>> Prov. 27:5

The ear that hears
> the reproof of life,
>> abides among the wise.
> Prov. 15:31

In the end, people appreciate
> frankness more than flattery.
> Prov. 28:23

CONTENTS

SECTION I	THREE STORIES	
	The Trophy	1
	A Love Story	33
	Saint Malo	43
SECTION II	OBSERVATIONS	
	Salt,—and Pepper	
	The Treasure	55
	The Formula	55
	Bible Study	57
	Conversation	58
	God's General Rule; God's Specific Rule	60
	God's Process	63
	"...The Spirit Giveth Life."— Not License	65
	Tomorrow	71
	Where are You?	73
	Forgiveness	77

Normal Condition of the Christian	79
A Twenty-cent Lightbulb	81
Five to One Odds	87
Healthy, Wealthy, and Wise	89
Giving	95
To Each His Rainbow	99
From a Sailor's Logbook	
Check Your Premises	101
Assertions	101
Attention	103
Blessing	103
Communication	104
Infinite Power of Unity	106
Too Much Credit	109
More Spiritual?—Or Less	110
Treasure in Earthen Vessels II	111
The Rest of God	113
The Written Word	115
The Loneliness of Command	117
The Question	119
God's Family Order	121
The Ratio	127
They Two Shall Be One	131
I'll Give You Gold	137
Contrasts	139
The Perfect Marriage	143
November 10, 1989	147

	To Tithe or Not to Tithe...	149
	Change	155
	Gold Beach	157
	A Story	159
	Reality	165
	She Called Me "Dad"	169
	The Ultimate Exhilaration	171
	Beginning	177
	Wendy's Story	179
	Healing Rest	189
SECTION III	**CHALLENGES**	
	Hath God [Really] Said?	193
	Adultery in His Heart	197
	God's Order	203
	God's Perfect Order	205
	A Harsh Opinion	209
	One Hundred Boats for the Philippines	217

ACKNOWLEDGEMENTS

Although it was my wife, Ramona, who urged and urged me to go to the healing sands of the Oregon Coast and "write those words that come from Him," I must also state my deep appreciation to three people who might be surprised at how their few words encouraged me.

Marine Attorney, Tom White, Chief Legal Rat of the Loyal Order of River and Wharf Rats, would, from time to time, read some of my "writings," and say, "Dean, you continue to amaze me."

And Leon Willis, President of the Full Gospel Fellowship of Churches, and his lovely wife, Latena, said, in effect, "Dean, keep sending those 'writings' up to us. They touch our hearts."

If this book does no more than challenge our thinking, does no more than make us examine our convictions, our concepts, yes, even our faith, and thus settle us more firmly in that faith, it will have done its job.

And thank you who are reading this book right now.

Jesus *IS* Lord.

Section I
THREE STORIES

THE TROPHY

Chapter I

The Questions

A three-foot high trophy, nicked and scarred from 19 years of battle over its temporary ownership, The Alaska Governor's Cup is not the America's Cup. But for Alaska, it is a sailing prize that has challenged small boat sailors to give their best, and it has challenged them for 19 years.

The mass of the trophy is wood, with two brass columns, one on either side, topped by sailboats, one, a Skipjack, and the other, a Laser, both remarkable little sailing machines. On top of the wood is the golden cup, and on top of that, a glorious angel, spreading his wings to heaven.

And on the face of the wooden block is a brass plate, with the engraved names of the 18 yearly winners before me. But how did it all come about; what were the series of miracles that have brought me to Roseburg, Oregon, this day in September of 1984, as I joyously carried that beautiful thing into a shop to have my own name engraved below the others as champion number 19?

Where should this story begin—at my birth on the Yakima Indian Reservation? No, not there.

During my childhood along the banks of the mighty Columbia River, and my youth and young manhood upon those waters? Yes, it began there, as a knowing and loving Lord poured into my soul, with the wind and the washing waves of that great waterway, a love for, an abiding affinity for the floating things that move upon the waters.

But this story is not an autobiography. It is a story of a sailing trophy, and how it came into my hands. And so this particular story begins forty-some years after that childhood and youth.

On February 19, 1972, after several years of some terrible storms, ripping, and roaring, and rending through my life, I surrendered that life, totally, to the Lord Jesus Christ. No, there were no flashing lights, no bells, no trumpets, at least not here on earth. But my life changed, or, in boating terms, those a sailor would understand, it took a whole new course.

Three and one-half years after that major course change, I found myself, after a 12 year absence, again working for FAA, the Federal Aviation Agency, as an Air Traffic Control Specialist, Grade GS-7, Step 1.

"Yes, Mr. Nichols, we know you have a home in Anchorage, but we must treat you as a *new* employee. You must take a field station, and then bid back into Anchorage in a year or so."

I was fortunate (or graced by God?) to get Homer, a fishing village, 220 miles by road, but only 110 miles by air, southwest of Anchorage.

But Homer is on the spectacularly beautiful, 30-mile deep Kachamak bay. With its sharp and rugged snow and glacier capped mountains, standing tall out of the sea, with its deep and often hidden fiords reaching back beneath the peaks, with its beaches, and forests, and coves, of unique beauty, and with its bounty of seafood waiting for harvest—Kachamak Bay is, beyond question, a boating paradise. I had to have a boat; and yes, a sailboat.

Calling from my childhood and youth, came the memories of a small boy and his German Shepherd dog, sailing the mountainous seas of the Columbia, (Oh yes, they have been measured at over 22 feet) and sailing there in a four-foot wide, twelve-foot long barge, with 1 X 12s for leeboards, an oar for a rudder, fir saplings for mast, boom, and gaff, a chunk of brown canvas for a sail, and a piece of quarter-inch manila rope for a main sheet.

But that little ship really sailed.

Making perhaps as much as 4 knots, on a broad reach, in 25-knot winds, we sailed across that mile-wide river, up its broad course, and down its stormy width. When that flat bottom came off those huge waves and struck the water again with thunder, the legs of that Shepherd, standing in the bow, would quiver like steel springs; but he stayed right there. And the young captain laughed, and yelled, and sailed for more.

Tugboats called the young captain, and the little sailboat drifted into memory. For 20 years, the work of the tugs, and the barges and logs they towed, built, with the merciless demands of the waters, a deep and abiding knowledge of seamanship, that curious, blending of practical knowledge with the indefinable instincts that read the weather, the wind, the current, the wave, and turn those elements into friends. And seamanship is seamanship, whether the driving power is a diesel engine or the energy of the wind, captured by the curving sails.

But airplanes, and their magic wings, the wonder of radio, the lure of the last frontier, these also called, and in 1958, Alaska became our home.

And so it was, in late winter of 1975–76, that I was on the long road from Anchorage back to my work in Homer. In the previous fall, we had seen a lovely little sloop, an Aquarius 21, at a boat show. I had fallen in love. A week before this day of revelation, I had been to see the dealer. They did not have an A-21, but did have an A-23, for nearly $11,000. I didn't have the money.

My wife was keeping our home, and her job, in Anchorage. So we had the costs of two homes, plus the costs of frequent travel and telephone calls. We just didn't have the money.

In my now four years as a Christian, I had heard much about giving, about faith pledges, about the miracles that come as the principles are practiced, but I wasn't thinking of those things this day. I was just debating within my mind, as I drove that long road, whether I should commit myself to support, on a regular basis, a Christian School, a concept truly dear to my heart. Suddenly it seemed so clear, yes, I can do that, I will do that, I will make that pledge.

The contract was only between my Lord and me, in my mind and heart; but it was real. I was at peace. So I just sat back and watched the moving drama of this part of Alaska passing by.

The Trophy

Several miles down the road, a voice spoke to me. No, it was not an audible voice, but the words were very clear, "You are going to get your sailboat."

The message was so clear that I found myself arguing, "How? We're going behind now, keeping two homes, all the costs... How?"

But the words came again, clear as a ringing bell, "You are going to get your sailboat." But I just laughed, and drove on, and soon forgot about it all.

My checks were deposited directly into the bank, but each bi-weekly pay period, we received a computer printout of our pay status. An 8½ x 11 sheet of paper, it was filled with numbers: grade and step, gross pay, taxes, net pay, annual leave used and balance, sick leave used and balance, and many other statistics. It took a while to read them. A week or so after returning to work, the Station Chief brought out our printouts. He always read them.

"Good Grief, Nichols, it looks like you got a raise, a substantial raise."

We crowded around to see. Yes, the gross pay for the two weeks period was over $2500. Even with $1000 income tax, the net pay was over $1500. My regular pay was a fraction of that.

I had been on the payroll since re-hiring, six months earlier, as a GS-7, Step 1. Study showed the sheet as stating:

Grade GS-9, Step 5.

"Well," I said, "I *was* a GS-9, Step 5, when I left, 12 years ago, but, yes, I reckon you'd better call payroll."

A half hour later, the confirmation came. "Mr. Nichols *is* a GS-9, Step 5, and should have been from date of rehire. Someone missed a Civil Service regulation that states that when one rehires into a job with the same qualification requirements as the one he left, and in which he had career status, he must be rehired at the old grade and step. The extra money is the back pay due him. His monthly pay is now that of a GS-9, Step 5.

My sailboat.

Chapter II

Fresh Water

But my spirit expressed caution. I waited a day, and then phoned a friend in the Credit Union.

"Marshal," I asked, "If I were to buy a sailboat, could I get the money?"

"Of course," came the ready answer, "how much do you want?"

"Well, I have the down payment. I'd need about $9500."

"Alright, give me the particulars on the boat, and I'll write it up."

"Not so fast, old friend, how much would the payments be?"

"Two hundred and five dollars a month; that's for three years. Shall I write it up?"

"No—no," I cautioned again, "Let me think about it, and, pray about it. I'll call you."

Ten years later I read a book by Loren Cunningham, founder of YWAM, Youth With A Mission. His book was titled, *Is That Really You, God?* On this day, ten years before, I found myself spontaneously following the great principle he had discovered, that is, praying and then waiting on God for direction, and then waiting on Him further for confirmation.

So I dropped to my knees and prayed, "Lord, if this is really of you, if I am indeed to use this opportunity to buy that sailboat, I want to wait a full week, seven days, before I phone the boat dealer. If the boat is still there, then I'll go ahead with the purchase." I fully believed that, if it was indeed His will for me to have that boat, He could and would hold it there for me.

But He did even better than that. Exactly seven days later, I picked up the phone, took a deep breath, and called the dealer.

"Rae," I said, "This is Dean, do you still have that A-23?"

She laughed a curious, short laugh, and said, "Well, yes, we do. Actually, we sold it a week ago, and the fellow towed it away. But two days ago he brought it back. Couldn't arrange the financing, he said. So yes, today, we have the A-23."

I was silent a few moments, then took another deep breath and said, "Well, you've just sold it for good."

"You want it?"

"Yes, will you call Marshall Ellison at the Fedalaska Credit Union; he will confirm the financing; I'll send the down payment from here."

I put down the phone, and just stood there in awe, and joy, and wonder, and looked out my window at the surf, from the ocean swells, crashing on the shore a couple hundred feet away, and I watched an eagle gliding along the cliff, on the soft ribbon of the wind, in his never ending hunt for food. I saw the blue sea, the scattered clouds, gracing a clear blue sky, and the small surface waves from the steady S.W. breeze. A perfect day for sailing. God is so good; He loves us; and He gives gifts to His children.

A year passed by, so swiftly, as time has its way of doing. But we sailed together every month of that year, and nearly every week, there, in Alaska. We grew to know, and understand each other very well; intimately is a better word. Sailing so much alone, I was forced to develop techniques for handling main sheet, jib sheet, and rudder in a smooth and swift sequence that, like any long-practiced game, became a finely tuned skill. There are no arguments, no discussions, no coordination required, when one man is the entire crew. That little sailboat and I truly became one.

But always, I took our Lord with me, and shared with Him the exhilarating joy of the beauty of those curving sails, turning the wind, and putting that strong tug on the lines that pulled us along; we shared the soft sound of the water rushing by the hull as we sliced up a bay just offshore from a gravel bar on which seals and birds were resting, fearless of this silent thing, so swiftly gliding by.

I remember, one glorious day, thanking Him again, as I so often did, for this marvelous gift. "Thank you, Lord," I said, "for this lovely sailboat. And you know, Lord, You can have it back any time You want."

But this day, something spoke to me; and I changed my prayer. "That isn't quite right, is it Lord?"

He did not speak, but I can still see His eloquent smile; His gentle waiting.

"I think, Lord, it would be better if I said it this way, 'Thank you for letting me play with your sailboat today.'"

And again, the flooding peace was mine; the glory, even if but for a little while, of walking in His perfect will.

And for six more years, He "let me play" with His sailboat.

In January of 1977, an opening came at the International Flight Service Station in Anchorage, so I put in my bid and was chosen. I would be living at home again and that was good. But as I settled that little ship on the cradle of her trailer and started to pull them both out of the water, the seductive cry of the salty sea sounded in my heart, "Do not go sailor, do not go little ship. There is freedom here, and challenge, and adventure, and there is love. Do not go, do not go."

But we are practical beings, even though the altar of practicality can be so ugly. And so we drove for Anchorage, and that silent, little vessel, her mast down, her sails furled, even her heart at rest, followed meekly behind, as a captured animal, bound and subdued, waits for the captor's next command.

About 60 miles, by road, north of Anchorage is a series of lakes, joined by short channels: Big Lake, Mirror Lake, Flat Lake, and Lloyd's Pond. The last officially named after our son who was lost at sea in 1966. We had a cabin on Lloyd's Pond.

And so our little ship found water again. Fresh water, this time, but she adapted well. The series of lakes are over 10 miles long, and 1 to 3 miles wide, with a hundred bays, and coves, and channels, and islands. It was not the sea, but it was sailing country, and that little ship and I became closer still.

I joined the Alaska Sailing Club, with its 20 or 30 racing rigs. I couldn't afford to own a racer *and* my cruising boat, so I raced the A-23 on handicap, as fair a way as possible to equalize the difference in boats, so that the skippers are more or less evenly matched. I knew my boat and sailing, but I didn't know such competitive racing. It took awhile. But in 1980 I won third place in the Governor's Cup Regatta over the Labor Day weekend.

But the winds on that inland lake were not like the strong, sea breezes. They were light and often variable. Everything is relative, of course, but relative to the 12-, 14-, and 16-foot racers, my 23-foot cruiser was a "big boat." In less than 4 or 5 knots of wind, we could not turn or accelerate as rapidly as the small ones, and at less than 2 knots we were nearly dead in the water. We needed 6 to 8 knots to fairly compete. But we had fun, made many fine friends, and learned a great deal.

The next year I won the Sportsman of the Year Award. That was a very real, very humbling honor, but it was not first place. I really wanted to win first place, even if just one time; for I knew I could, if I could just have the winds.

But God has His own, curious way of bringing things about.

Chapter III

A Team Again

In 1982 I sold that little A-23 to a fine man, who later became a beloved friend; and with a very ill wife, moved out of Alaska and down to Roseburg, Oregon. And no, Alaska did not let us say goodbye without real tears. A year later my wife crossed the bar on her own eternal voyage. I was alone, far from the sea, and although this is a garden land, to a sailor, it is a desert; I was hard aground, and no tide to lift me off. So I waited.

But a year and a half later I was given a new wife, and a new life. And she, who had known a terrible shipwreck, found a new husband, a new marriage, a new ship, and a Captain to take command.

And now begins our story.

I had kept my membership in the Alaska Sailing Club, mostly for nostalgic reasons I suppose, but as 1984 moved on, I was unable to obtain a receipt or acknowledgement of my payment of dues.

Ramona is a North Dakota, Swedish, farm girl. They grew up with a "Do-it-or-shut-up" attitude. It takes some getting used to, but it is a good attitude.

Big Lake, Alaska.
The Sailing Club in the upper right and
Lloyd's Pond in the lower center.

When I grumbled about the lack of response on my dues, and then threatened, with less than full meaning, to go up there, borrow my old boat, win the Alaska Governor's Cup Regatta, and demand my membership card in person, she called my bluff. And the next thing I knew, I was phoning my friend in Anchorage.

"Jerry, I have to come up and try for the Governor's Cup one more time. Is it possible you could have the A-23 at Big Lake for the Regatta?"

And his immediate answer, "Of course. She'll be at slip 14, Burkshore Marina. You have a key."

I called the travel agent for reservations.

I had not sailed that boat, I had not sailed at all for two years, and arrived in Anchorage barely two days before the races. I found the old trailer, hauled her out and cleaned her dirty bottom as best I could, and, because her new owner, my good friend, Jerry, is such a packrat, unloaded a thousand pounds of gear. And then I drove myself into less than two days of intensive practice. But the rusted skills came back surprisingly quickly, and by Saturday, the first race day, we were a team again. It was like I had never left her.

Saturday morning was nearly still, as I motored into the Club. The members were surprised to see me, but most offered a warm welcome. A bit later, Les Brattain, the Commodore, came to me and said, "Dean, some of the little boat skippers are grumbling about your "big boat" stealing their wind. We are going to start you five minutes early.

I thought, "Uh huh, change the rules without warning." But then I remembered that Sportsman of the Year Award, and said aloud, with a genuine grin, "OK."

There is a white flag; five minutes later a blue flag, and five minutes after that, a horn and the red flag. Go! I was to start on the blue flag. We started sailing and jockeying for position. Just before the blue flag, a light breeze came up, and as the flag hit the top of the pole, we scooted across the starting line, tacking for the windward mark. The breeze was fading. As I rounded the mark, the horn sounded, and I looked back to see the entire fleet of 20-some boats, in nearly a flat calm, struggling across the line. With another light lift that the fleet was missing, I was around the second mark and heading for home before the first boats made the first mark. We not only made first place on corrected time, but in actual time as well.

The next two races were essentially the same. But all were so slow, we had to quit for the day with only three of the eight-race series run. I had two firsts and a second, an enviable position; but Cups are not won on breaks alone.

Ordinarily the Regatta is run on Saturday and Sunday, with Monday, Labor Day, as a Club play day: Challenge races, kids races, swimming and picnicking. But for some reason the Race Committee elected to make Sunday the play day. It was well; as there was no wind. I won a challenge race by drifting around a one mile course in just over an hour. The other boat finally gave up.

My daughter and her husband, who had flown to their cabin for a weekend, had loaned me their house. Alone that evening, I started thinking seriously about my chances of winning that Cup. But I needed wind, and more specifically, from the N.W. at 6 to 8 knots. So I called a friend in the Weather Service. "Margaret," I asked, "What are the winds forcast for Big Lake tomorrow?"

"Oh, Deano, no winds at all; no change at all."

"But Margaret," I protested, "I need wind if I'm going to win that Cup. And I need winds from the N.W., and at 6 to 8 knots. Higher would favor me, but lower would favor the little boats. From the N.W. at 6 to 8 knots, Margaret."

"Oh Deano, I'd like to help you, but sorry, no winds for tomorrow."

I stood in that lovely, silent home for some time after that and looked out the big windows and watched the yellow path of the moonglow shimmering across the water. I thought about all the hunger and torment in this world, and asked myself, "With all the hurting people on this earth, does God really care if one man, who would be 65 tomorrow, would win a coveted sailing trophy on his birthday?"

And then I dropped to my knees and prayed, "Lord, I really don't know if it is cricket or not to pray to win; but you said you would give us the honest desires of our hearts. And I really do want to win that Regatta, if only this one time.

"But Lord," I cried, "I want to win it honestly. I've practiced for years, I've cleaned up the boat, I've done all I can; but I must have wind. If it be in thy will, oh Lord, may we have wind tomorrow from the N.W. at 6 to 8 knots, and for the full five races?" I felt fully at peace, went to bed, and slept soundly.

Chapter IV

An Unusual Wind

Monday morning, the final day: It was cool, a light frost on everything. When I got to the boat, the lake was a mirror; fog hid all but the closest things. I started the motor and ran the two miles to the Club. The fog had lifted by then, but the lake was a placid pond.

"Oh Dean," the Commodore said, "We want you to start today with the rest of the fleet. That gave you too much advantage Saturday."

It didn't; and I also thought to myself, "Fine, change rules in the middle of the game." But I remembered again that Sportsman of the Year Award, and truly grinned and said, "OK."

Nine thirty, Skippers Meeting, the lake flat calm.

Nine forty five, breeze picking up, from the N.W.

Ten A.M., the white flag is up, and whipping in a N.W. breeze at 6 to 8 knots. There were no clouds, no reason for that N.W. wind. But it stayed that way for the rest of the day.

In my prayer Sunday evening, I had promised to let the Holy Spirit be my Navigator. But as we jockeyed for position on the first race, I forgot my promise, and fought with the rest for that best starting position. I had a lousy start, nearly the last across the line. But with that relatively stiff breeze, for our little boats, it was a close race all the way. I made third place on corrected time.

But on the next race, I remembered my promise; and as we sailed back and forth, waiting for the red flag, I listened for the Navigator's voice. The only place I found peace was on the inshore end of the line, the soft end. There was less wind for starting, and I would start on a port tack. But there only I found peace.

The red flag was up, the horn sounded; the entire rest of the fleet took off across the line on a starboard tack, every one having right of way over me. As I drove for the middle of the pack, there were still several boats trailing. If they did not change tacks, I would be forced to turn down wind to clear them, losing precious seconds. But as that "big boat" bore down on them, they all changed tacks, lost a few seconds, and we charged by them in a flurry of spray.

And from then on it was serious sailing. *No* unnecessary moves in the boat, *no* unnecessary changes in sail trim, *no* unnecessary moves of the tiller—sail the shortest course possible. I talked quietly to myself, like a coach to his player, "Steady, steady. Do you have the mark abeam; no, hold another 500 feet. Now, turn for the mark."

By then, most of the fleet was on a port tack, and I on a starboard tack, all heading for the mark. All would have to give way to me. As we rounded the second mark, and headed for the finish, two or three of the really fast ones were ahead.

I knew that, with this fast time, the lead boat would have to beat me by three minutes in actual time, to beat me on corrected time. As the first boat crossed the line, and the horn sounded, I hit my stopwatch. Three minutes or less to go. My breathing quickened, my heart pounded, but the coach in me kept talking, "Steady, steady, don't worry about that Laser; keep your eye on the mark; no wasted moves."

Two minutes and 20 seconds later, we crossed the line. Another first place.

With such good winds, we ran the last three races in a very short time. And each time, my secret Navigator had me start from that oddball position. The fleet never did catch on.

There was a protest meeting; there is always a protest meeting. And then we milled about, waiting for the race committee to work out the numbers. The N.W. wind continued to hold at its steady 6 to 8 knots.

Finally, a voice boomed over the bullhorn. "Gather round, you sailors, we have the winners." Curiously, I was not anxious. I did not know if I had won or not, but I was at peace. The A-23 and I had sailed a good race; we had made few mistakes; we waited.

Starting with 7th place, a name was called out. A man stepped forward and accepted his certificate. I was certain that we had done some better than 7th place.

Sixth place was called, and then fifth, and fourth, and third. I think then, I started to hold my breath. Second place was called, and then time stood still.

Gary Rogers, the Vice Commodore and Race Committee Chairman said, casually, "I think you have noticed that there is one name we have not yet called." A long pause. "Dean Nichols, come and get your Trophy."

In that brief, silent moment I realized that I had known, quietly and confidently, even before I boarded that airplane, 2000 miles away, and five days before, that this was the way it would be. Still, the emotions were there at the very edges of my eyes as I stepped forward and took that rugged old Cup in my arms.

I had, somehow, thought that the Cup had to go back to Club Headquartes, but others said no, I could take it home. Les Brattain, the Commodore voiced some reservations, "I don't know; it has never been out of Alaska before."

"Oh," I said, "I'll care for it like a treasure; I'll treat it like a baby; I'll carry it in my arms like a child."

He called the Vice Commodore over, "What do you think?" he asked.

Gary too was torn between my ebullient assurances and their own concerns. But the next thing I knew, both men just walked away.

Close friends stepped up and said, "Dean, take that Trophy down to your boat and get out of here."

I protested, "But I was going to help clean up."

"Take that Trophy down to your boat and get out of here."

So I obeyed. Doesn't the Good Book say, "Listen to the counsel of good friends."?

The sailor, his ship and his trophy.

I wedged the big Cup on the cabin sole, between a bulkhead and the centerboard well, cast off my lines, pushed the bow out to catch the wind, trimmed my sails and rushed away before that N.W. wind, still holding at 6 to 8 knots.

But the story does not end here.

Chapter V

The Answers

I rushed "home" to share the victory with my daughter. "But Judy," I said, "I promised to carry this thing in my arms. Do you have an old blanket I can wrap around it?"

"I have better than that," she answered, "I have a new, king-size blanket. We don't have a king-size bed, and you do."

So we wrapped that huge blanket around an already large Trophy and tied it with a piece of rope. I called it "my baby," but it was now the size of a small child.

But in the early dark of the next morning, I drove to Anchorage International Airport, parked my daughter's car in long-term parking, and carried my suitcase and sailor's duffel bag to the terminal. I was an hour and a half early. Diplomacy takes some time, I have found.

I walked up to the Wein Air Alaska counter and asked if I could leave my bags while I went back for another. It *was* awfully early, I knew, but the reluctant growl of approval didn't sound good. I prayed again as I walked back out into the dark night for the Trophy.

And when I came back in, I realized I was not at the Wein counter; it was the next one down. So I put on my most confident grin, walked up to the counter and asked, "Would you girls like to see my baby?"

It was early; there was time, so of course they wanted to see. And then, of course, I had to briefly tell my story. "But I promised," I told them, "that I would carry this thing in my arms, all the way to the States. Are you going to let me do that?"

"Oh, wow," said the girl, "I don't know; do you have your ticket?"

I produced my ticket.

"Dean Nichols," she remarked, "I used to know a Dean Nichols."

"Oh," I answered, "where, when?"

"Oh, it was so long ago, it couldn't have been you."

"Well, maybe," I countered, "where, when?"

"Well, years ago, my father-in-law worked at FAA; he worked with a Dean Nichols."

"I worked at FAA here in Anchorage; what is his name?"

"Lloyd Patterson."

"Lloyd Patterson," I exclaimed, "I worked with Lloyd; he was one of my closest friends."

"Then you are that Dean Nichols. Hey, just a minute," and she got on the phone to Crew quarters.

A few moments later she came back. "Don't worry about a thing, Dean. A stewardess will tuck your baby away in the crew locker. It will ride like it's in a baby carriage."

The Trophy

There was some difficulty at the security check point, and I couldn't really blame them; but I insisted, correctly, that I already had approval from the front counter, *and* the crew.

A half hour later we stepped aboard, a smiling stewardess, her eyes wide as I pulled the blanket back to show the gleaming gold, said, "Hey, don't you worry, we'll tuck your baby right down here." I walked back and settled in my seat.

But still the story does not end.

I had a plane change in Portland; and more, it was to a Sweringer Metroliner, a lovely little airplane, smooth, turboprop, pressurized cabin, but also very small. "No carryons, please."

But, one step at a time.

We were late getting out of Anchorage. The connection in Portland would be close. As we taxied up to the unloading finger, I noted that I had only minutes to spare. I retrieved my ungainly "baby" from the same smiling stewardess, and ran, as best I could, up the concourse, frequently shifting this "sleeping child" higher in my arms. I rushed to the Horizon counter. "Can I still make flight 101?" I asked.

"Oh, I don't think so, but let me call the gate."
"Yes, if you hurry, they can take you." She didn't seem to notice my huge carryon, as I rushed away.

Her voice called after me, "There is a message for you at the gate counter."

"I'm Dean Nichols," I told them, "You have a message for me?"

"Yes, Ramona says she'll be late. Do hurry for the gate."

"That's OK," I called back, "I'm going to be late too."

The young man at the gate noticed only that I was having difficulty with my burden, and helped me fumble for my ticket, pulled the coupon, and directed me down the steps.

"One more hurdle, and we're in," I prayed, as I walked out across the tarmac.

A tall, athletic looking young man was taking carryons and stashing them in the nose compartment.

I walked up to him with as big a grin as I could muster and said, "Hey man, you want to see my baby?" I pulled the blanket back, exposing that glorious angel, and the gleaming gold Cup.

"Hey man, where did you get that," he asked, stopping all motion for a few moments.

"This, my friend, is the Alaska Governor's Cup Sailing Trophy. I just went to Alaska and took this thing away from those guys. I get to keep it for a year. But hey, man, this baby is fragile; can you treat her like an eggshell?"

"You bet, man, I got a special place, right back here in the tail. I'll pack some soft bags around her. I got her, man."

And I knew he had, and climbed aboard.

Ramona met me in Eugene; I held her in one arm as I carried that evidence of triumph, unwrapped now, of course, in the other. We claimed my luggage, leaped into her car, and rushed for a victory dinner in Roseburg.

And now, a few days later, I am climbing the steps to that trophy shop and asking the questions:

A weary but victorious sailor home from the sea.

How did this all come about? What were the series of miracles that had brought me to this place, this day to have my name engraved below the others as Champion number 19? Well, we have read the story.

But what are the conclusions? This is not a "religious" magazine; but neither is this a "religious" story. It is a narrative of facts, evidence, at least to this sailor, that there is a God, and He does indeed, work in the lives of His people. Those are my conclusions. The reader can draw his own.

But, taking my conclusions, then well might one ask, "Why would this God give one man a sailboat, and then the winds with which to win a 'graven image,' a wood and metal trophy, while there are starving ones in Ethiopia?"

But then one must also ask, "Who is man to question God? Who is man to doubt that He is well able to lift one man from a mountain top and place him on a cloud, at the same time He is lifting another from a muddy swamp and placing him on solid ground?"

One man needs a test of endurance and faith, so he struggles with the miry clay. Another needs a test in humility, so he struggles with the temptations that come with wealth and power and honor.

But through it all, the Great One speaks, "Whether in sickness or health, authority or servanthood, riches or poverty, victory or loss, walk with Me, and walk in glory."

I, myself, have known all of the above; but this story tells of one time when, on a tiny sailboat, I found indeed, that it is absolutely glorious, even if but for a little while, to find oneself walking in perfect harmony with the will of God.

The Trophy

The sea, the sea, the endless sea
sends out its siren call for me.
Yet oh that call, that haunting call
cannot be heard by one and all,

But only by the hearts attuned
to sense the mysteries it holds,
to feel its healing for my wound,
to hear the challenge to the bold.

A challenge that is not a dare,
but rather invitation there
to see your soul stand tall and free
while held with awe of the endless sea.

Dean Nichols

A LOVE STORY

Alma was something special.

Oh, "Of course," I hear you say, "She was your wife of 43 years; she raised three beautiful children for you; she was physically beautiful, and worked at staying that way; she loved to keep house and garden; plants and people clearly loved her, and responded to her. Of course you would say, 'She was something special.'"

But let me tell you her story.

She was married to me, Dean Nichols, in Vancouver, Washington in 1940. She was sparkling, and beautiful as 17-year-olds can be. We were "in love." Oh, but what the years had to teach us about love.

We are all framed or guided by the social patterns of our times, and for our time, the pattern was good, and we followed it. I worked hard at being a good provider and father; and Alma worked as hard, or harder at being a good homemaker and mother. As nearly 40-year-old "baby" Jo Ann recently said so simply yet so eloquently, "She was the best mother."

Oh yes, we sinned against each other, often in word, mostly in attitude, but even sometimes in deed. But our greatest sin was that of most marriages, I think. We gave up, here and there, as time grew into years, and just quit trying to hammer out the differences. It became easier to just bury them. After all, the good times, the joys of sharing a family, the growing old together, weren't they vastly more important than hammering on differences?

And so we built a marriage, bracing around those differences so cleverly that the world saw only a strong, good marriage. But down deep in our souls, we saw the flaws buried there, and, to our credit I suppose, we knew they did not belong there.

It was in Anchorage, Alaska, October, 1980. Alma had had a flare up of diverticulitus. Dr. Billings had prescribed an antibiotic. The soreness and inflammation went down. We relaxed. But a blood test showed an abnormality that he wanted a colleague to check. Dr. Hale ran some tests and then said, "I think we have CML, Chronic Myelogenous Leukemia, but I'd like you to see a hematologist." We did, and he confirmed, CML.

"Well," we asked, "What is the prognosis?"

"Without treatment, you have three years. With treatment you will have four and a half years."

We elected treatment, and yet, less than three years later, we laid her to rest. They did their best, they really did their best, but the best of medical science was just not good enough. The only "treatment" available today for this condition is chemotherapy, which is much like "treating" one's garden with a spray and hoping you kill more weeds than lettuce or tomatoes. I only hope that medical science, through the beautiful young men who tried to help her, learned all there was to be learned from this great loss.

The day will come, I know, when medical science, and the people, will look back upon this day often in the same way we look back upon the blood-letters where, when patients did recover, it was in spite of medical "treatment," and not because of it.

But we can't dwell on all that; this is a love story.

Back in February of 1972, after surviving the most devastating marital storm of our lives, we realized the blunt truth of the Bible, "It is not in man to direct his ways." So we did, in truth, formally, and deep within our hearts, turn our lives over to the Lord Jesus Christ.

Of course our marriage was not suddenly perfect. After 32 years, the flaws were so perfectly encased in their cells that, I suppose, if we noticed them at all, we thought they were pearls. Still, way deep in our souls, we knew we did not want them there.

But back to the last three years. The long, cold winters of Alaska, so exciting in our youth and good health, became increasingly difficult to bear as her strength and vitality so slowly, almost imperceptibly, ebbed away. We knew, much as Alaska had become our home, still, we knew we had to move south.

We tried to transfer down with FAA. We made several trips down, looking for a new home. Through the years I had dreamed of spending my own "golden years" near the sea where I could touch and see and smell and hear the sea and those marvelous, floating things that ride upon her. But as the search continued, I began to learn, as I can see so clearly now, the lessons of selflessness, the very foundation of His love, that He was teaching me.

Almost countless little barriers blocked our choice of this place or that. The months turned into years. I retired from FAA in Dec. 1980; and still the search continued. Mostly in deference to her brother, Ted, we agreed to "check out" the Roseburg area; and the pieces fell into place, firmly, easily, with almost a perfect fit. We had found our new home; and in June of '82 we moved down.

It is lovely here, the winters mild and easy, the summers stimulating to us and to the growing things she loved. My wife was content. Oh, it is a hundred miles from the sea, but my wife was content. And I, I was almost surprised to find what God has been trying to teach mankind for 2000 years, that giving, sacrificing for another, and especially for the other half of one's life, was glorious. Accomplishments for ourselves can be fun, satisfying, even joyous. But giving, when given with God's love, is glorious. But I'm getting ahead of my story.

Instead of the sailing machine that still cruised, quietly, back there on the sea of my dreams, we bought a travel trailer, and made a trip or two. We loved it. Alma loved it.

She had always wanted to see this great land, this land so clearly blessed by the God she loved, but to see it from a little closer than 30,000 feet. So we promised daughter Jo Ann in Pennsylvania that we would start back on March 8, cruise east through the southern states, spend two weeks there, and then, as the snows melted away, return through the northern regions of our land; —our land.

On March 7th we put her in the hospital. A few weeks before, some undulating fevers had begun.

Several days later, blood tests showed that, although the white cell count was high, the platelet count was seven to eight times above normal. To blast the platelets with enough chemotherapy to bring them down, would bring the white cells to a dangerous low, or wipe them out altogether.

Our beloved physicians suggested P32, a radioactive phosphorous injected directly into the blood stream. Her body would store the phosphorous in her bones and thus, in effect, localize the radiation against the bone marrow, the only place where platelets are formed. If they got the dosage just right, the platelet count would be brought to normal at the same time that the half-life of the phosphorous brought the radiation to an insignificant level. The white cells would be less affected, since they are produced also in other parts of the body.

So on February 24 we took the treatment and continued plans for our trip with growing enthusiasm. But the fevers slowly worsened, she had dehydrated badly, and on that Monday of March 7th we put her in Mercy Medical Center. No amount of testing could determine for certain the cause of the fevers, and they continued to drain her. But the devastating discovery, as the blood tests continued, was that the guns of radiation, firing steadily into her bone marrow where friend and foe alike were being blown away, continued their work far beyond the plan. Her white cell count came down to as low as 200, against a normal of nine to twelve thousand, and her platelet count to as low as 1000, against a normal of around 300,000.

As the repeated 13-day half-life of the phosphorous did its work, the guns died away, but with no white cell soldiers for defense, or platelets for clotting, she was clearly being kept alive by God's grace. Medical science was helpless, and we really felt for them in their helplessness.

And now begins our story.

Of course we believed in divine healing. We knew of too many cases of such healing to deny it. But we also knew that God is sovereign, and even more than healing, we wanted to be fully in His will.

One day, near the end of that first five-weeks hospital stay in March and April, I walked into her room. Alma asked me to pray with her for something. We had, of course, known about God's great love, ever since He swept us into His Kingdom, that day we surrendered to Him. But she said she wanted to know His love in a deep, personal way; to be intimately aware of the wonder of His love.

So I closed the door, we talked over our intended prayer, and I knelt beside her bed. We asked to be so filled with His love that it would overflow from us, even with no effort on our parts. We asked to be so filled with His love, that others would no longer see those "nice people," Dean and Alma, but see only His love. "And Lord," we cried, "As much as we want healing, even more, we want to know and be filled with this love."

Of course, as Alma has often said, God never does things the way *we* plan. We actually had the mild audacity to expect that one or both of us would have a vision, perhaps, and see Jesus, and buckets full of His love would be poured into us, and she would be gloriously healed, and we could just continue our normal lives with His great love flowing out from us everywhere we walked.

But He chose to teach us, show us, fill us with this love through shared suffering; and with that, the marvelous revelation of the infinite value of shared suffering.

Into the second week of April we brought her home. Her blood counts were still precariously low, but holding. "The radiation has run its course," the Doctor said. "It is up to Alma now to start building blood again."

With her having almost no white cells, it was my task to give her shots of antibiotics every eight hours, help her keep track of a number of medicines and, when the fevers soared too high, to lay cold, wet towels over her burning body for an hour or so until her temperature came back down to an acceptable 102 degrees or less. We finally settled on taking her temperature and giving her Tylenol every three hours around the clock. With the limited area for the shots, it became increasingly difficult to find an unbruised area where those 1½-inch needles would not hurt so much.

But I was amazed to find my own strength holding, even increasing, strength that I know was not my own. Compassion and patience far beyond my known limits were there, and Alma gave so much of herself to help me. She didn't have Leukemia, we had it; she was not fighting those devastating fevers, we were. A oneness was becoming ours that we never dreamed possible. And through it all, we watched the unimportant things of life wash away, and out of the silent storm we saw love grow.

We didn't have to confess, in spoken words, our sins against each other. They were all washed away in the flood of that great Love, and we saw each other, clearly, deeply, with no shadow or veil or space between us, and we loved, with a Love beyond words.

If I were to give others any counsel at all from this experience, it would be, "Learn, oh do learn the art of selflessness toward your life's partner now. Do not wait; oh let me urge you, do not delay this deepest of God's lessons. It is not a burden, it is a gift from God, a gift, a gift."

Alma rallied some at home, even walked, slowly, but she walked out to her beloved art studio and did some painting. We took a couple trips with our lovely travel trailer, and made it out to dinner a few times. Our beloved Physicians experimented with two more options, megadoses of vitamin B6, and Lithium. But the B6 only appeared to aggravate the devastating fevers, and the only apparent result from the Lithium was an even more rapid breakdown of her capillary walls. We can only believe now, that she had an appointment on the other side; and that appointment would not be denied.

So on June 15 we were back in the hospital, knowing, deep inside, that unless our God directly intervened, as He most assuredly can and does, we were on the last mile of the trail home.

A few weeks earlier I had met, through circumstances so unusual that it had to be God's plan, a lovely Catholic couple, Anthony and Sylvana Amendola. Aren't those beautiful names. I had told them of Alma's desire to know God's Love in a full and intimate way, and of our prayer. I have never known such lovely Christians from whom such love flowed. He had had a vision of God's Love, and ministered in churches, Catholic and Protestant alike, teaching about God's Love. And Sylvana had a ministry teaching women on the healing of memories, even memories buried so deeply they were hidden from conscious view.

They had come to our house one evening and gave of themselves for an hour or so. The effort of listening, and responding, drained much of Alma's fading energy supply; but when they left, she knew that she had been touched by God's Love. Exhausted as she was, and though I hurt for her, we both knew that what she, and I, had received was worth that terrible price. When we started our last mile there at Mercy, we knew "from whence cometh our strength;" we were ready.

I had a cot in her room, and so shared her every cry and even her last struggle for breath. So it seemed, at the time, so understandable when, driving home to freshen up one day, I saw with a clarity I cannot adequately describe, the answer to the world's most pointed question, "If this God of yours is so great, why does He allow so much suffering?"

And the answer, "We can know love by sharing good things, even joys, but if we want to know the unfathomable depths of God's Love, we must share suffering." Alma and I found that Love, and we saw it overflow to others around us.

There were nurses there, strong and confident and capable, who, though not toughened or calloused, did have their emotions carefully folded away beneath the years of service to others.

But on the day my beloved wife grew too weary to breath any more, and her brave and precious heart began its eternal rest, those lovely angels of mercy cried.

In her own desperate questioning, my daughter, Kathy, asked one of those nurses, "How do you bear this day after day?"

And her answer, "Well, first, it doesn't happen every day; second, we don't get to know most people that well, but here? Now? Alma was something special."

> "And this is My commandment; that you love one another as I have loved you."
> John. 15:12

> "Husbands, love your wives, as Christ also loved the church, and gave Himself for it."
> Eph. 5: 25

IN MEMORY OF
Alma June Nichols

BORN
June 26, 1923
Ilwaco, Washington

PASSED AWAY
June 20, 1983
Roseburg, Oregon

FUNERAL SERVICES
2:00 p.m.
June 22, 1983
Chapel of the Firs
Sutherlin, Oregon

OFFICIATING

Pastor Don Franke
Dr. Anthony Amendola
MUSIC
Mrs. Pat Kahl

FINAL RESTING PLACE
Valley View Cemetery

SAINT MALO, *CITÉ CORSAIRE*

I have walked among men, real men. And the catalyst of such association stirred up in my being a keen awareness, a vibrant joy of seeing my own self as a virile, male animal.

The 41st Annual Congress of the *AMICALE INTERNATIONALE DES CAPITAINES AU LONG COURS CAP HORNIERS* (roughly translated, International Fellowship of Master Mariners of Cape Horn) is over. Grand old men of the sea, and I who closely follow them, will wait another year before we meet again. *Most* will meet again. For some will cross the bar before that day. The merciless hound of time who chases the four winds will catch them at last.

But here in this truly fabled city, the city of the French Corsaires, and fifty-three years ago, a group of men met to form a simple organization. Their common ground? They had battled the storms of Cape Horn in commercial sailing ships and won.

Cape Horn: That southern tip of South America, jutting southward, southward into the Antarctic, forcing ships down into that meeting place, that battleground of storms; forcing them, that is, if they would sail on to Australia, or Japan, or the west coasts of the Americas, or the paradise of the South Pacific islands.

Many are the stories of challenge, and victory, and fear, and loss, and victory again. And these men are living evidence of those victories.

On May 20, 1985, the 41st Congress convened, again here in St. Malo. I, through some curious move of the Spirit, was here as an honorary member of the American Section. Although the official membership category, Sympathetic Member, would be more accurate. Capt. Frank Rizzo, head of the American Section, had invited me to go to the Congress. I recognized at once a rare opportunity, and claimed it.

I had arrived three days early in order to get my bearings, scout the beachhead, and absorb the character, the color, the spirit of this walled city with its narrow streets, cobblestones, high, steep-roofed buildings, all of stone, and the whole arena dripping with history.

But my close association with these men of sinew, of fibre, of iron, began almost immediately. Checking in with the International Secretary, Jaqueline Ailett, I was invited to a cocktail hour the next evening aboard the sailing-training ships, *Etoile*, and *Belle Paule*, as guests of the French Navy.

Jaqueline had spent most of her early childhood in California, so was a charming combination of the lovely, and gracious French Lady, and a delightful California Girl. "You must have a written invitation," she said. "I will send over a written invitation." A few hours later, I was accosted in my hotel lobby by a gentle giant of a man, 77-year-old, Capt. Jean

Perdraut, President of the French Section, hosts to this year's Congress. He had personally hand carried my "written invitation." I was beginning to see the magnificent stature of these old sailing Captains.

The next morning I found the two 130-foot topsail schooners moored to the quay a few blocks from my hotel, and Capt. Perdraut aboard talking with an officer. "What dress for tonight?" I called over.

"The best dress as possible," he called back. "In the Navy, always the best dress as possible."

So out came the dark blue blazer, black tie, grey slacks, and polished black shoes. Boarding promptly at 1830 hours, I properly saluted the quarter-deck, the officer on watch, and called out the question, "Permission to board Sir?"

"Permission granted," and the salute was returned.

Capt. Perdraut greeted me and introduced me to his wife and another 78-year-old Cape Horner and his wife. We chatted a bit, and then, as the crowd gathered, I just moved about, inspecting the ships and closely observing this unique gathering, here in this very special corner of the world.

About 50 people only came aboard, and I was the only American, or even English-speaking guest. But they were all very gracious to me. Sailors busied about serving hor d'oeuvres and a dozen different drinks. When I asked for wine, the sailor didn't understand wine, or *vino*, or chablis; but an officer across a table called over, "You want wine?"

I grinned and said, "A French ship, and no wine?"

He grinned back and said, "Oh, we drink wine with meals, but not here."

"Oh, am I improper then?"

"No, no, of course not." And wine was brought up from below.

But the brief happening that poignantly impressed upon my spirit that evening came as the gathering just started to disperse. Standing next to the beautiful young man, the present Captain of the *Etoile*, I too saluted as the very first Captain of that lovely ship was piped ashore. Fifty-three long and stormy years had worn upon his frame since that day, and that grand old man, now in his late eighties, had some difficulty getting up the steps to the gangway. But once ashore, he turned, stretched up several inches, and saluted. My God, what a man. Tears of deep, deep respect brimmed at the corner of my eyes. I told the young present Captain, "That touches one's heart." He said nothing, just nodded with very, very evident understanding.

And so was the evening for one American aboard a sailing ship as a guest of the French Navy; and then, walking back through the small portal in the wall around this medieval city, City of the French Corsaires, to my room in a stone castle.

Monday, May 20, 1985: A very brief day, in this story, a story of sharing with salt-encrusted men of a day now gone by. But there have been rich experiences during this brief hour that have driven their golden arrow deep into my soul.

The welcoming ceremonies were held at the Palais du Grand Large, a beautiful, new convention center outside the walled city. Only two hours, from

Saint Malo, Cité Corsaire 47

5 to 7 P.M., but there were many absorbing conversations with some fascinating people. Even my seat partner was a lovely, Swedish woman, who, after her English warmed up, developed a British accent. She and her Captain-husband had spent some years in Scotland, and the mixed accents showed it. She was later to be one who poured a healing balm into a spiritual wound I was to receive. But more of that later.

There was a wonderful conversation with two Australians, husband and wife, and a short visit again with 69-year-old, Capt. John Aage Wilson. I had met him earlier in our hotel, and had brought him to my room to give him notes on the schedule of events. We had such a brief time together, but what a life he has lived: scoundrel, Captain, owner of a tug fleet, husband of three wives, and Captain of the last commercial sailing ship of record to round Cape Horn in 1967—as late as 1967.

But during the brief hour of the welcoming ceremonies, I discovered what was to become the theme of this entire Congress as it touched deeply into my heart: There is something wonderful about these men, a very real, a very evident manliness about them; the living beauty of God's finest creation, the manliness of real men.

Tuesday, May 21: Quoting directly from my journal we read, "This last eight hours have been at least a week in experience. How do those amazing computers we call our minds process all the data? How do those powerful engines we call our emotions maintain a stable cruising speed when they are charged with such energy laden fuel?"

The French, I believe, are especially rich in their ability to make any ceremony dramatic, deep, and alive. And so they did at the Flag Raising Ceremony in the courtyard of the Palais du Grand Large promptly at 9:00A.M. A French Marine Band, smartly uniformed, played for us; and then, on a piped signal from a Navy Bos'n, the flags of 14 Nations went up in a semi-circle around the already raised official flag of the A.I.C.H., *Amicale Internationale Cap Horniers*. And there, third from the right, rose Old Glory. Our Flag, my God, what a magnificent, soul-stirring sight; our Flag. And I found myself wiping tears, unashamedly from my eyes. Surely those who are not deeply stirred by that glorious symbol of our homeland, especially while one is standing on foreign soil, have something tragically lacking in their beings.

And then the noble assemblage of around 250 grand, old Captains, with another 200 or so of their ladies, plus a number of honorary members, such as myself, walked back through the portal in the town wall, and a few blocks through the narrow, cobbled streets to the Cathedral for the Memorial Service for those who had crossed the bar in this last year.

It was a huge building, even perhaps a magnificently architectured cave, dark, even dank, but most impressive. As we sat on the cold, hard, wooden benches, the sun was pushing through the stained glass windows a hundred feet away and reaching 80 or 90 feet from the floor.

Because it was almost all in French or Latin, it was a long one-and-a-half hour service, (however impressive and clearly recognizing man's very real need of a Savior) and it was quite cold—no heat at all in that stone, stone building with even a stone-block floor. But I most surely noted no irreverence as we moved back out into the sunshine. It could have been more physically comfortable, but it was mandatory within our souls that we pay our last respects to the 12 to 15 mighty men of the sea who have gone to Glory before us.

Then followed a reception by the town Mayor in the open-air, high, stone-walled city hall courtyard outside the city walls. The acoustics were excellent, and there were many, very moving presentations. At the meeting, Capt. Rizzo gave to Capt. Perdraut, a copy of a proclamation by the City of Elkhart, Indiana, U.S.A, proclaiming this day, May 21st, 1985, as Cape Horner's day there. Capt. Perdraut said later, "I was deeply touched."

The large assemblage then moved back to the main ballroom in the Palais du Grand Large, for the Official Banquet. Capt. Rizzo and his lady friend, Gerry, were assigned to table 25 with the Italian Section, and I to table 32, which turned out to be a combination of U.S. and Belgian, except that I was the only American.

But they were truly, truly delightful. As the precious lady next to me said, "Oh, we all have to speak at least three languages, native Flemish, French, and English, and some Dutch and German. She, herself, spoke quite good English. We had a wonderful time.

And we truly dined. Nearly four hours of course after course, efficiently delivered by beautiful, young people to nearly 600 guests. The acoustics here were terrible, at least at our end of the huge room, so we missed most of the speechmaking; but we were having great fun. Mady, my older and portly seat-partner, was an excellent conversationalist, and easily kept up a running dialogue with me in English, *and* with others in both French and Flemish. We talked of the sea, and international relations, and the sea, and politics, and the sea, always the sea, and the many lives the sea has taken, and yet the very life the sea has given to mankind.

Finally, by about five P.M., the meeting melted away, and I walked the seven or eight minute walk back through this city, through this living stone, ringing with the music of history, to my room.

This last eight hours have been at least a week in experience. How do those amazing computers we call our minds, process all the data? How do those powerful engines we call our emotions maintain a stable cruising speed when they are charged with such energy laden fuel? As Mady and I agreed, why did two such people as we spend 60 or so years, a lifetime, thousands of miles apart, and suddenly find ourselves at a table in this historic, seaport city, dining on duck, and wine, and champagne, and finding an unending flow of things to share in conversation? And then we simply agreed again, "God's Process." Don't resist or question His Process, but watch it unfold, in awe, and be glad.

Thursday, May 23: A busy, full, but sadly, a somewhat disturbing day. We were going home. And yes, we know, the glorious glow of camaraderie that had us enveloped for this last week had to fade—of

Saint Malo, Cité Corsaire

course it did; but it is disturbing that I have not been as successful as I'd like in rejecting the attack on me and my country delivered by a Swedish Cape Horner as we were speeding away from Rennes, a train transfer point.

He recognized me as an American. "When did *you* sail the Horn?" he demanded. So I told him, of course, that I haven't, yet, but rather was here as an honorary member of the American Section. But that only rallied the scorn of a few others. "American Section? Where are you going to get the members? You had the Panama Canal."

Of course I was completely taken off balance, and can think now, a day later, a dozen ways I could have handled the whole situation much better. But after three or four of them ganged up on me against my spontaneously organized defense, "Surely in all the U.S. we can find a dozen Cape Horners," I just backed off and quit, and just sat and thought.

But across from me, and a seat back, sat the lovely Swedish lady who had shared with me during the opening ceremonies. And with her sat her Captain husband, a giant of a man, kind and strong. We shared the delight of some multi-lingual children who had come aboard the train. Both, but she especially, poured the healing balm into my wound. "There are some purists in the organization," she said, "who believe that *only* "real" Cape Horners should be members; that when the last one dies, he must first go to St. Malo, sign the log, and *then* cross the bar."

When we left the train and parted in Paris, I told her husband, "The man who was unhappy with me because I was not a "real" Cape Horner? Tell him, without us 'Sympathizers,' at the next Congress, there will be no one there to honor you."

He smiled a kind, gentle, but most understanding smile, touched me on the shoulder and said, "Of course, of course."

I felt much better, the glow was restored, and I rushed to my taxi for the mad ride across Paris to Gare L'Est, and the Express train for Luxembourg and my plane home. I was leaving France, St. Malo, and the great men of sail. My life has been changed. How better can I say it all than to quote from the Homily delivered at the Memorial Services in that great Cathedral back there in St. Malo:

"Thus you were baptized with the small quantity of water that we use in our churches, but also, like St. Paul, in the furious water from which life must be snatched...

"Others show their courage differently. But sailing the way you did is, in the extreme, a witness to mankind...

"Glory to God alone, *Soli Deo Gloria*, as John Calvin says. The glory of God, as well Calvin knew, is shown in the courage of men who have shaped the history of mankind.

"Our acknowledgement is due to all those whose effort went to the extreme to show that God created man to be responsible. It is not for nothing that the Captain is referred to as 'Master, after God.' One must carry this responsibility and show that what God created is still alive."

Section II
OBSERVATIONS

I realize that to some, "Thus saith the Spirit of the Lord," may sound "Churchy," or "Religious." But I assure you, I would say it not at all for either reason. If I were to add it to any of the "writings" that follow, it would be simply to disclaim any authority, or responsibility, for what I truly feel to be profound declarations. For I am absolutely certain that they were given, for me to write, by the Holy Spirit.

And you? You have the full right, of course, to judge the declarations, and apply them to your own lives, or not, as the Holy Spirit may direct.

But I urge you to not treat any of them lightly. Condensed in those few words are volumes.

Dean Nichols

SALT, —AND PEPPER

The Treasure
(2 Cor. 4:7)

We all carry some burden of "the earthen vessel," and if we are not very careful, or better, if we are not spiritually discerning, we can miss the "treasure" *God* has placed in every Christian; even in ourselves. The "earthen vessel," though so very evident, is nothing; the "treasure" is all.

The Formula

There are, relatively, only a few places where the Bible speaks directly, and specifically to a specific problem. Generally we can say that the Bible is a mathematical formula, not a line item instruction book, especially in the area of daily living.

Take the electrical formula, shown sometimes as a circle formula. Draw a circle; divide the circle horizontally; divide the lower half vertically. In the upper half, place a W (Watts.) In the lower left place an A (Amperes.) In the lower right, place a V (Volts.) One can then read either, Watts over Amps equals

Volts; Watts over Volts equals Amps; or, Amps times Volts equals Watts. The formula is infinitely variable, yet it is always, always, precisely true.

The foundation for the perfect formula of the Bible is, of course, Love. One time we may give a hug, another time we may chasten, or counsel, or listen, but always, always, love.

One person may read a certain scripture, and find it applying perfectly to the problem he is facing. Another may have a totally different problem, at least in man's understanding and yet read the same scripture and find it applying perfectly.

We are not talking here of "interpreting" the scriptures differently; we are not talking of wresting the scriptures to make them say what we want them to say. If the electrical engineer tried to do that with the circle formula, he would blow every fuse in General Electric. It is no wonder then, that we get into deep trouble when we try to alter, even minutely, that Great Formula, the Holy Bible.

But we can believe, safely, truly believe, that if God wants one of us to produce so many watts of spiritual power, He can, by His Sovereign Will, decrease the Amperes, and increase the Volts, or increase the Amperes, and decrease the Volts, so that the power comes out just as He planned.

The Bible *is* God's perfect formula.

Bible Study

"Bible Studies" are too often, too much. We too often let them turn us into Scribes and Pharisees, arguing the "points" of the law, bringing strife.

Jesus said, "I will write my laws in your hearts.... I will send you a comforter... *He* will [instruct] you."

Bible studies should always be led by a competent instructor who has done his homework, his research. That one should be the Pastor, or one who is *clearly* being led by the Holy Spirit. Otherwise, Bible study should be in private after preparatory prayer for guidance and revelation by the Holy Spirit. We *must* let the Holy Spirit apply the "formulae" of the Bible, gently, and sweetly, to the particular problems we are trying to solve.

Preaching, on the other hand, words from the pulpit *should* startle us once in a while, or even often. If every word that is spoken there brings only our nod of approval, or our nod, our amen, or even our hallelujah, we are receiving nothing new. Yes, Jesus truly said, "I am the same yesterday, today, and forever." But do we fully, completely *know* Him? Do we Know the *fullness* of His commandment to Love? Preaching *should* stimulate us, even prod us, to deeper study of, and correction in our walk with God.

There is true Bible Study, and there is true Preaching. It is up to us, listening to the Spirit of Truth, to judge each as we share, and listen. If we experience stimulation mixed with peace, not complacency, peace, *then* we can rightly judge that we are being led by God's teacher, God's preacher, or by the Holy Spirit. Otherwise, we should get out; we are not in a proper Bible Study.

Conversation

It has been written: The secret of conversation is building on what the other says, not in countering what they say. But the secret is also in responding to, or acknowledging what they say, not in dismissing what they say so you can have your say. Response, acknowledgement, is the key.

Oh, we can differ from another, as long as it is sincere difference, and does not simply counter them, or worse, dismiss what they say. An honest difference is at least responding. Paul stood against Jesus, against His disciples, strongly, but he *was* responding, with honest, firm conviction. He was not just *countering* in order to make the pretense of conversation.

Of course, what the other says, does, and indeed should, act as a catalyst in setting off our own mental processes. Don't you remember? The most fun conversations we've had are when one adds a point to what the other said, and then the other adds a point, like two skilled workmen, adding building blocks (ideas) to a structure; fitting pieces into a puzzle.

And of course, sometimes we may correct the other; but when the correction is built on the general statements of the other, there is no loss of face, nor should there ever be. We build, on what the other says.

And also, instead of guiding, or counseling another, we too often drive, or run them, as we would a child—a subtle difference, but a crucial one. Doesn't the Devil himself operate on subtleties? He never hits us straight on. But we are getting away from conversation.

Oh, the Proverbs are full of counsel on conversation: Proverbs 1:5, "A wise man will hear, and will increase learning...." 3:30, "Strive not with a man without cause...." 4:20, "My son, attend to my words; incline thine ear unto my sayings." 10:31,32, "The mouth of the just bringeth forth wisdom, but the perverse tongue shall be cut out. The lips of the righteous know what is acceptable, but the mouth of the wicked speaketh perverseness." 12:25, "Heaviness in the heart of man maketh it stoop, but a good word maketh it glad." 13:3, "He that keepeth his mouth keepeth his life, but he that openeth wide his lips shall have destruction." 15:1, "A soft answer turneth away wrath, but grievous words stir up anger."

And more: Proverbs 15:4, "A wholesome tongue is a tree of life...." 18:4, "The words of a man's mouth are like deep waters, and the wellspring of wisdom like a flowing brook." 18:13, "He that answereth a matter before he heareth it, it is folly and shame unto him." 23:16, "Yea, my heart shall rejoice, when thy lips speak right things." 25:11,12, "A word fitly spoken is like apples of gold in pitchers of silver. As an earring of gold, and an ornament of fine gold, so is a wise reprover upon an obedient ear." 31:26, "She openeth her mouth with wisdom, and in her tongue is the law of kindness."

There are many, many more, and we have not even looked at James. But clearly, conversation, real conversation does not just happen, *it is built.*

God's General Rule; God's Specific Rule

There is a crucial difference between these two, and failure to discern the difference can get us into deep trouble.

Meekness, for example, is one of God's general rules. Generally, we are to take punishment, even unjust punishment, or mistreatment by another, meekly. Let God, or someone else correct them.

But rarely, very rarely, I might add, He will use us to do the correcting. God is Sovereign; He can set in motion a specific rule, that may appear to override His general rule, anytime He chooses, because He sees the end from the beginning. He knows factors in the overall equation that are far beyond the comprehension of our finite minds and hearts. But there is danger here. There is temptation; and temptation is danger.

I remember one time being badly mistreated by a fellow employee. It went on for some time. Finally, in frustration, I found myself telling him off; or perhaps, in less worldly terms, rebuking him sharply. It worked—well. Later, I looked to God for forgiveness, even correction; but all I received was His definite nod of approval. In that *specific* case, I was the best one to rebuke this man.

But the temptation? The danger? Sometime later, an identical (or so it seemed) situation arose. "Ah," I thought, "this is exactly the same as before. I'll tell him off." But the Holy Spirit was shouting in my ear,

"No! No! No! That was a specific rule you received last time; you have no authority this time; you operate by God's general rule unless you *clearly, clearly* receive a specific rule."

All of 1 Corinthians Chapter 12, deals with God's general rule: He gives gifts to His children. But the specific rules are, To *one* is given [one gift]... to *another* is given [*another* gift]...and to *another* is given [still *another* gift.] [Author's emphasis.] And these *different* gifts to *different* people (specific rule) make up the body (general rule.)

The Israelites had God's general rules, "Thou shalt not kill..." for example, yet in Psalm 106:34, they were rebuked by the Lord for failing to obey a specific rule, "*Destroy* the nations."

In 1 Samuel, Chapter 15, they were commanded to "...slay both man and woman, infant and suckling, ox and sheep...." A specific rule. But they failed to discern. They mixed general rule, Sacrificing to God, with the specific rule, "Slay all," and so were rebuked of the Lord, "...Behold, to obey is better than sacrifice, and to harken than the fat of rams."

There are many, many examples we could give, as many, perhaps, as there are people.

But *the* rule to remember is that, there *is* a crucial difference between God's general rule, and His specific rule. Let us endeavor always to discern that difference.

August 1986

GOD'S PROCESS

It is God's process that counts. His process must and will proceed. Whether illness or health, win or lose, death of an ant or a flower, or order or suffering or victory, all are part of His process.

If we *strive* for healing when His will, His process calls for suffering or illness, we oppose His process, and will not have peace. But also, if we endure illness or suffering when it is His will, His process for our victory or health, we oppose His process, and will not have peace. We conform to His will, His process, or live outside of His peace.

Those who talk to plants and animals know that there is no resentment or hurt when they are cut, crushed, or even killed within God's process. So whether we live in riches, luxury, or fatness in America, or suffer and die of starvation in Ethiopia, is of no *direct* consequence. All that really matters is, are we in tune, in harmony with His process? *Only there* is peace.

Pricks or goads:
        Don't kick against. Acts 9:5
Wages, or fringe benefits:
        Be content with. Luke 3.14

Freedom:
> Of course, take it if the opportunity comes; but otherwise be a slave or servant who serves his master well, faithfully and with love. 1 Cor. 7:17-24

Giving:
> As the Holy Spirit directs—no less, but no more. 2 Cor. 8:12,13.

April 1985

"...THE SPIRIT GIVETH LIFE"—
NOT LICENSE

"Who also hath made us able ministers of the new testament, not of the letter, but of the spirit; for the letter killeth, but the Spirit giveth life."

2 Cor. 3:6 (King James Bible)

A few years ago, a man was driving on a city street. Several hundred feet ahead, the roadway dropped away, so that one could not see if another vehicle were approaching in the opposite lane. Of course, there were double lines in the center of the road to signify, "No passing; No crossing of those double lines."

Suddenly a small child darted out from behind a parked car and into his path. Seeing that he still had a couple hundred feet before the brow of the hill, and no approaching traffic in sight, he swung his car violently to the left, around the child, then quickly back into his own lane. The child, apparently realizing that he had done a wrong thing, darted back and vanished.

A thousand feet or so further back, a policeman in a patrol car noted the erratic movements of the car ahead, turned on his flashing lights, and apprehended the driver near the bottom of the hill. The policeman never saw the child. He cited the driver for the obvious violation of crossing those double lines.

"But the child," the driver protested.

"I saw no child," the officer responded, "But I did see you cross those lines, and that is a violation of the law. See you in police court," and wrote out the ticket.

Fortunately, a neighbor, looking out his window, saw the whole drama, including the child's sudden appearance, and as sudden disappearance. The neighbor willingly appeared in court with the driver, and verified that indeed, the child had acted as the driver had said.

"But the law spells out, to the letter, that you can *never* lawfully cross those double lines," the Judge intoned, "Are you aware of that?"

"Yes, I am, Your Honor;" the driver responded, "But in my defense, may I state an assumed premise, the spirit of the law, that, especially in such a case as this, the purpose of the law is to protect life?"

The Judge agreed.

"Then may I further state in my defense, Your Honor, that, had I obeyed the letter of the law, a child would have been killed. Although I did violate the letter of the law, I obeyed the higher, spirit of the law, and a child lives."

The Judge dismissed the case.

Yet, as Christians, we too often discard all (Scriptural) law, by saying, in effect, "We are no longer under the law, but under Grace." And then we go on and act as if we have license to do as we please.

But in the above quoted Scriptures, and story, it is clear that we are not under just the spirit, but, the spirit of the *law*. Didn't Jesus say, "Think not that I am come to destroy the law...; I am not come to destroy, but to fulfill."? And, the Holy Spirit said in Hebrews, "...I will put my laws into their hearts, and in their minds will I write them." Write what? His *laws*.

"Oh, if I just love everybody," one protests, "I'll be alright." That is right on. But it hangs on that tiny, but *enormously* significant word, "if."

When Jesus was asked which is the most important commandment, He answered with the well-known duo, in paraphrase, "Love the Lord with all your heart, and your neighbor as yourself." And then He made this astounding statement, "All the other commandments, and all the demands of the Prophets stem from these two laws, and are fulfilled if you obey them." Matt. 22:40, Living Bible.

"...*All* the demands of the Prophets..." If, if, if.

No, no, we are not free of the law. We are free of the Letter. We are free, because we are the slaves of the lawgiver, Jesus.

An excellent example of the Letter, is "Tithing," but which, under Grace, becomes "Giving." The freedom under the Spirit is really *His* freedom. But, as we have said, since we are *His* slaves, we are free under *His* freedom; that is, He knows our financial condition *far* better than we even think we know it. That is why He can tell us—if we are really listening—tell us, often to our astonishment to, one time, give nothing; and another time to give 100 percent;

one time to give five or ten percent, and another time to give 50.

Clearly, clearly, the rigidity of the *letter* of the law was just that, too rigid, too cold bloodedly demanding. But the spirit of the law gives the Holy Spirit the freedom of flexibility. And when we truly trust Him, we will find ourselves truly "hilarious" when we give. Isn't that the Word, "God loves a 'hilarious giver.'"? We will have that "merry heart that doeth good like a medicine." And then the money (or time) will do great good, because it is wrapped in a Spirit of Joy.

Some time ago, I had given, to a lady, a copy of a written prophesy entitled, "God's Family Order." As we were having lunch together, she referred to the first two Scriptures, Genesis 2:18—"And the Lord God said, 'It is not good that the man should be alone; I will make him a help fit for him.'"

And, Genesis 3:16—"Unto the woman He said, 'I will greatly multiply thy sorrow and thy conception; in sorrow thou shalt bring forth children; and thy desire shall be to thy husband, and he shall rule over thee.'"

She then countered them with the statement, "But that was under the curse; we are now under Grace."

It was clearly evident that in that one counter, she totally threw out the page and a half of Bible quotes on the same subject that followed—all from the New Testament. She appeared to be effectively saying, "The Curse has been lifted; we are now free of 'submission,' free of *any* family order ordained by God."

No, no again; we are *not* free of the law. God still has a family order. It is just not to be lived under the rigid *letter* of the law, but under the gentle persuasion of Love; but still, *His law*.

Oh yes, we have the liberty of the spirit, but, yet again, "...only use not liberty for an occasion to the flesh..." Gal. 5:13.

It is not our freedom but His. And only because we are His, is it our freedom too. We surrender to Him; we love as He commands; He writes His *laws* on our hearts. The Spirit indeed giveth life, not license.

Bastendorff Beach
January 22, 1989.

TOMORROW

Tomorrow, my love, tomorrow;
the storm is but for today.
The clouds and the dark, and the sorrow
are blessings, if only we pray

And trust Him to turn the storm's fury
to a steady, broad-reaching breeze,
the clouds to a fresh, cleansing shower,
if only we stay on our knees.

And the dark He will turn to the morning
with the light from a new day to see
that our way is a bright sea before us;
His gift,
        inviting,
                and free.

For prayer turns the grief and the sorrow
to comfort; His Word says it's so,
if we will but wait for tomorrow,
and trust Him,
        and trust Him;
                I know.

                For Ramona
                Faisalabad, Pakistan
                January 4, 1984

[Read slowly, even methodically.]

WHERE ARE YOU?

Bastendorff Beach
The Oregon Coast
August 10, 1988

Yesterday I was in the driver's seat of my big Chevrolet Suburban and towing my Coachman travel trailer over Highway 138 on my way to Bastendorff Beach Park on that fabulous Oregon Coast. The car weighs 6,500 pounds, and the trailer about the same. That is over 6 tons of steel, and plastic, and rubber, and wood, rolling along a paved road that was well engineered, and carved right through the stony mountains. I "knew" where I was.

I was poignantly aware of my physical location, as the light touch of my fingers commanded that 6 tons of marvelous machinery to respond. We were driving down a solid road that I could so plainly see before me, and that was clearly marked with mileposts, and signs, and centerlines. I "knew" where I was and where I was going.

But suddenly, I was as poignantly aware of a piercing question, "Where am I?" It took some deep re-examining to re-determine the *true* answer. But let me give that answer by asking you:

Where are you; right now, where are you?

"Oh," I hear one answer, "I am sitting in my car, in a parking lot in Anchorage, Alaska, on a Thursday afternoon, and reading your story."

Or another says, "I am at home, at 682 Page Road, in Winchester, Oregon, in the evening, and reading your story."

Or another says, "I am riding a Northwest Airlines DC-10, seat 23B, at 37,000 feet, over the State of Iowa, and reading your story."

And I say to these: obviously, all of you are reading my story; but none of you have told me *where you are*.

Good Grief, people, we must think. Your physical location, or perceived location, is not "where you are." This physical world is not reality. Reality is eternal, and obviously again, this material world is *not* eternal.

God's Word says that the very heavens one day shall be rolled together like a scroll; the elements shall melt with fervent heat; this body will return to the dust from whence it came. But you, your spirit will continue on. God will continue on.

"And *this* is life eternal that they might know Thee, the only true God, and Jesus Christ Whom Thou hast sent."

The only reality is God, is the spiritual. And so your location can only be denoted in relation to Him. In very truth, your physical location means nothing at all. Whether at home, in your car, or in a plane, thousands of feet up in the sky, these are not, "where you are."

Where are You 75

Always, when we are asked, "Where are you?" we answer by giving our location in relation to a known place. But if the natural world, the physical, is not reality, then again, our answer has no meaning, no meaning at all.

But if God is the only reality, and certainly He is, then the only answer we can give that can have any validity, would be our relationship to Him, and to Jesus Christ Whom He has sent.

If you don't know where you are in relation to Jesus, then, my beloved,
>> you don't know
>>>> where you are.

(This declaration is very condensed. To grasp its full depth, it must be read slowly, thoughtfully, and perhaps even several times.)

FORGIVENESS

Forgiveness is hard work. At best, it is hard work; and then, when we are asked to forgive one who has not asked for forgiveness, has not at all repented, we find forgiveness sticking in our throats.

Surely love includes forgiveness, so when God commands us to "Love thine enemy," He is not asking, as some seem to require of us, that we minimize their wrong, or imply, by our forgiveness that there was no wrong at all. He is simply requiring us to do our part only. And what is that part? To place on deposit, in a trust account in the Bank of Heaven, our forgiveness. Then, when the offender goes to the Bank, presents evidence that he has met the conditions, the Trustee, God, immediately delivers the deposit.

Isn't that the way a trust account works on earth? If I am to pay you $1000 when you have met certain conditions, before you go to all the effort, and sometimes risk, to meet the conditions, you ask me to place the money in a trust account at a bank. When you have met the conditions, and ascertain so to the trust department of the bank, you are immediately given payment.

God is the only One Who can say, "If my people, who are called by My Name, will...turn from their wicked ways...*then* will I...forgive their sin...."

The one wronged, and the wrongdoer, can both trust God, whether they believe they can trust each other or not. When we deal through the Great Trustee, forgiveness is as it was meant to be, easy, a joy, a great release.

September 1986

THE NORMAL CONDITION OF THE CHRISTIAN

Many years ago I saw a lovely picture of a ship at anchor in a harbor. And the caption read, "A Ship in the harbor is safe, but that is not what ships were built for."

Several months ago, Pastor Don Franke and I were discussing his series of sermons on the normal condition of a Christian. And this statement, or prophesy came forth: "We do not endure the storms of life *so that* we can at last find a safe harbor.

"We rest in a safe harbor, refitting and preparing *so that* we can again challenge the storms."

A few weeks ago I read these words by Pastor Milt Atkisson, Missions Director for the Full Gospel Fellowship of Churches: "The stresses and strains of serving the needs of humanity must also have a balm so we can continue to meet the needs of others. That balm...is fellowship.

"The strain that is engendered in ministry needs something to fill the gap as we continue to engage the enemy and meet other's needs. Fellowship provides the rest, the R & R, that refreshes each one so we can continue in the work of the Lord. Our Fellowship has long engaged in this practice without defining its nature. God often sets in motion things that later he backs with the Word.

"Jesus, you know, had two towering sources of strength—one was His fellowship with the Father with whom He communicated frequently, and the other was the fellowship with the team members who journeyed with Him. We need both today."

Isn't it wonderful how God, Sovereign God, is telling the same thing, at the same time, to different people all over the world?

September 1986

A TWENTY-CENT LIGHTBULB

That's all I wanted; to replace a 20¢ lightbulb in the instrument panel of my wife's little car, a '78 Plymouth Volare.

The subject of a story? Good Grief; that was not at all my intention.

I had looked at it and couldn't readily see how to get the old bulb out; and besides, standing on my head makes me seasick. So I told my wife, "Take the big Chevy to work tomorrow; I'll just run the Plymouth into the Chrysler shop and get one of those skilled and agile young men to replace the bulb."

So the next morning I phoned Chrysler for an appointment.

"You bet," the Service Manager said, "Bring her in at 2:00 P.M."

I suggested, hopefully, "Shouldn't take one of those expert young men more than a minute to change the bulb; I just can't stand on my head to do that anymore myself."

"Sure," he answered, "That's generally the case; although once in a while they can be a real pistol."

I hung up the phone and thought about that pistol. I wasn't sure what it was, but a shadow, named "expensive," flitted across my mind and then left.

At 1:30, I drove the seven-tenths of a mile to the post office, shut off the engine, picked up my mail, and went to re-start the car. It wouldn't start. Or more correctly, it would start, but wouldn't run when I turned the switch to run position. That was curious; but it would not run.

So I walked that seven-tenths of a mile back to my house, called the Chrysler Service Manager, and explained my situation, and the way the engine acted.

"Any idea what might be wrong?" I asked hopefully.

"Sure," he responded confidently, "The spark resistor has gone out; happens every once in a while on that model. But it's easy to fix. There's a ceramic block about two by three inches, up on the firewall; you can't miss it. Cost you five bucks for a new one; take you five minutes to change it."

My 20¢ lightbulb was now over $5.00, and I hadn't yet reached the garage.

I phoned my brother, Ted, "My car is dead at the postoffice," I told him, "Gotta run to town for a part; can I borrow a car?"

"Of course," he cheerily responded, "You have your choice of four: a Jeep, the old Dodge pickup, the Buick, or the Cadillac."

I ran down the hill and through the woods to brother Ted's house. He met me with the keys to the Cadillac. "It hasn't been run in a while," he said.

I climbed in and started the engine; then rolled down the window, "Shultz, how far will this thing go with the gas guage on E?"

"Oh, it'll go a long way," he assured me, "You're OK." So I drove off.

But one just does not borrow another's car, and bring it back empty. So I dropped into a gas station on the six-mile trip to town, intending to ask for $5 worth of gas. But as the young attendant was walking up, the amount rose to $10, and before I spoke, I realized I was sitting in a gold Cadillac. "Fill'er up," I requested, feeling generous, of course. He did, and I signed the ticket for $23, and drove for the garage and purchased the part.

As I drove back for the Plymouth, I did my arithmetic. I had over an hour of time invested, had walked over a mile, and had spent now over $28, and that 20¢ lightbulb was still in the box at Chrysler. But it was a beautiful day in Roseburg, Oregon, and my sense of humor was still intact and running well.

I installed the resistor on the Plymouth in close to the five minutes the Service Manager had said, and started the engine. It ran perfectly. So I locked it up, drove the Cadillac home, walked back up the hill and through the woods to my own house and phoned Chrysler.

"As you know," I said, "I've had some delay. Can I still bring the Plymouth in for that lightbulb?"

"Aw, bring her in," he said, "We'll fit her in somehow." So I walked that seven-tenths of a mile back to the post office, and drove for town, and turned the car over to the shop.

I had made up my mind when I got out of bed that morning that this was going to be a good day; "power of positive thinking," you know. Nothing was going to get under my skin. So I wandered into the comfortable waiting room and sat down. It was now after 3:00 P.M.

I picked up a *Reader's Digest* and started reading. It was five years old, but I had not read it; and besides, some of the articles were very good. I was relaxed, and learning.

An attendant came out, "The fan belts are pretty bad, do you want us to replace them?" he asked.

"Sure," I answered easily, "If it needs it, fix it," and went back to my reading.

About 4:00 I checked at the counter. "No, Mr. Nichols, they're still working on it." So I went back to my comfortable seat in that quiet waiting room and picked up the other *Reader's Digest* there. It was only four years old, but, it too had excellent articles I'd never read.

Another hour later I looked up to see some workmen leaving. "Hmmmm," I thought, "It is after 5:00." So I checked at the counter.

"Yes, we just now have it here, Mr. Nichols; that will be $52.43."

For just a brief moment, I had to put a grip on my morning's determination to be "calm, cool, and collected" this day. But it came back, I paid the bill, took my keys and drove the car home, and reflected on a curious day. All I had wanted was a 20¢ lightbulb, but I had now used up over half a day, had walked nearly two miles, driven 25 miles, and spent over $80.00.

And I thought, "We get some curious cards dealt to us in the Poker Game of life, but I guess we just have no choice but to play them."

And then I looked over the work order in more detail, and sure enough, there, in the parts list: one lightbulb, twenty cents.

FIVE TO ONE ODDS

"My car quit."
  1. You have a car.
  2. You have a husband.
  3. He got out of bed to:
      a. Drive you to work;
      b. Start your car for you; or
      c. Loan you his.
  4. Nine hundred and ninety-nine times out of 1000 your car starts and runs well.
  5. It's a beautiful day.

"Naturally, I get the one out of gas."
  1. There was enough to carry you to work.
  2. There are service stations along the way.
  3. You have a credit card.
  4. Your husband would have driven you to work.
  5. It's a beautiful world.

"I'll be late for work."
  1. You have a patient and understanding boss.
  2. You can easily get all your work done.
  3. They'll notice you.
  4. There are other jobs.
  5. It was a very beautiful weekend.

Three negative and fifteen positive. Really, darlin', positives and negatives always stack up that way; and that's pretty good odds now, don't you think?

Anchorage, Alaska
May 26, 1970

HEALTHY, WEALTHY, AND WISE

God wants us healthy, wealthy and wise. Satan wants us healthy, wealthy, and wise. Two identical statements? No. One is truth; the other counterfeit.

So let us examine these two, very opposite statements. Let us first examine the Devil's desire for us, since it is ultimately negative, a lie, darkness, nothingness. Let us examine this first, that we might dispose of it and get on to the positive, the truth, light, substance, life.

Why would the Dark One want us healthy? Why, we can see the answer to that all around us. So often, we speak to one who is radiantly healthy, and he answers, "Oh, I don't need that religious stuff. That's for the weak, the sickly. I'm too busy living. I can take care of myself."

And why would he want us wealthy? Again the answer is all around us. "I buy what I need. I'm a self-made man. I was born into and for wealth. The poor? Sure, they need some "religion" to lean on, but that's not for me."

And what does the lying one mean when he would have us wise ? Why, what else, but wise in our own conceits. The very religion of Humanism is built on this lie. They say, "Since we are all a product of evolution, then, obviously, man is the ultimate intellect. Man not only can, but must solve *all* problems; man not only can, but must build his world; man not only must be, but *is* the ultimate authority. If you need a god, then look to man." And in their blindness, in their arrogance, even in their often very sincere faith, they miss the penetrating thrust of the rapier of God's word, "It is not in man that walketh, to direct his steps."

Why does the Devil want us healthy, wealthy and wise? Simply that by the use of deceptively seductive reasoning, he can lead us away from God, or build the simple barrier of our own wills to the sweet and gentle call of God. Oh yes, he wants us healthy, wealthy and wise.

But now let us examine the positive, the lifting will of God. Why would God want us healthy? Well first, that is the way He designed us. "In the image of God created He him; male and female created He them...." He loves us. Do not you as a father or mother desire, almost above all else, that your children be healthy? And the action of a superbly healthy, skilled athlete, is that not God's beauty and grace of creation in motion?

And there is work to do. The healthy body can do much work; and the healthy body and mind can work with very real joy. "My brethren, I would above all else that you might prosper and be in health..."

And so we look at wealth. Why would God want us wealthy? Oh, partially as a test, of course. Surely wealth is a far greater test of humility than poverty.

But with wealth, the committed Christian can be used by God to help the poor, to set up industry and provide jobs, to pay taxes that finance government. And with wealth God's beloved children can enjoy the gifts of fine cars, and homes, and sailboats, and vacations, and beach resorts, and cruises, and share these great enjoyments with our Lord; share them, as a grateful child shares a gift with his own earthly father.

But more than these two, God wants us wise. Over and over, through the Proverbs, the Psalms, in fact, through all of God's Word we are charged to seek wisdom, get wisdom, obtain knowledge and understanding that you may be wise.

And is not love, the ultimate wisdom? "Thou shalt love the Lord thy God with all thy heart...and thy neighbor as thyself."

On these two hangs all the law, and everything the Prophets said. [Author's paraphrase.] On these two hangs every charge to get wisdom, to learn love; oh my beloved, to learn love.

The entire Bible points to this one charge, to learn love.

Of course, we cannot reduce that infinite charge to these few pages. But we can touch a few of the instructions in that infinite textbook. And the first is: Do not disdain *any* method of God's instruction.

Do we learn patience when we are ill, and even when the healing processes, designed into our bodies, are obviously at work; slowly, but at work? Do we learn patience when we pray for healing of some chronic problem, and the evidence of healing is slow to come? Do we learn compassion for others in their illness, when we ourselves have passed through the "fiery trials that so easily beset us"?

Do we learn trust when we are struck by a financial problem for which we see no solution, and so must cry to God for help? Do we learn wisdom when friends and family are torn by strife and come to us for counsel?

Do we learn love, God's agape love, when friends strike out at us as enemies, and hurt us deeply?

So then, if so much is learned by all this suffering, why read the Bible, why pray, listen to sermons, meditate on things of God? Why? It is to load our mental computers to give the Holy Spirit data with which to work in our lives. Doesn't God's Word say, "Thy Word have I hid in my heart that I might not sin against Thee."?

We must have wisdom above all else, above even health and wealth. Yes, God wants us healthy and wealthy, but above all He wants us wise. So what do we do when physical, financial, mental adversity strikes?

Well first, every situation is a *new* situation. There is no pattern, or better, there is only one pattern, and that pattern is Jesus. "I am the way..." So we do not wrest the Scriptures, we do not make them say what we want them to say. True, they do apply differently in different situations, like a mathematical formula, but always, we let the Holy Spirit apply them.

"Don't I have a right to feel good?" you ask.

Beloved, you have no rights but the right of self discipline. "You are bought with a price; you are not your own."

Fill yourself with God's Word, and then listen to the Holy Spirit for instruction on healing, on financial solutions, on the settling of strife.

To one He may say, [Author's paraphrase] "What are you sitting on your duff for? Pick up your bed and walk."

To another, "Hold still while I anoint your eyes."

To another, "I will come and touch him."

To another, "Thy faith hath made thee whole."

Or to another, "My Grace is sufficient for thee."

To one He may say, "Tighten up your budget; care first for your family."

To another, "Change jobs."

Or to another, "Make a certain faith pledge."

But through it all, He is saying, seek wisdom, the ultimate of which is love.

May I speak a loving parody on 1 Corinthians Chapter 13?

"And now cometh health, wealth and wisdom, but the greatest of these is wisdom."

GIVING

Is For The Giver

God is sovereign.

He can feed, clothe, house, prosper anyone or any organization He chooses, whether or not you or I give. Obviously, He *chooses* to do most of His giving through us; but He does not *need* to.

Giving is much like praise. God does not *need* praise in order to lift His self-esteem; He *knows* Who He is.

As growing children, *we* need the approval (praise) of others to help us build our own self-esteem. (And we don't mean flattery; we mean true compliments or approval.) So we tend to measure God's *desire* for our praise by our own needs, our own measure.

But God's desire for our "hero worship," is that of any loving father who desires to see his child grow, to be perfected.

And so an earthly father, who has learned the right way, the hard way, and knows that his wife has also been perfected and purified through the fires of years, and affliction, tells his son to "Watch me; do it this way," or tells his daughter, "Listen to the counsel of your mother; do as your mother does." He does not do this to raise his own ego, or to flatter his wife.

He speaks to his children thus because he loves them, and desires to see his children grow, to be perfected.

He knows that, as a piece of clay, placed in a vessel, will eventually take the shape of the vessel, so a child will become like those with whom he associates, and especially like those he admires (praises.)

And again, giving is much like praise. God is a giver, and He knows giving works, tremendous works; some, in the life of the receiver, but infinitely in the life of the giver.

God has no needs; He owns everything. He is "able of these stones to raise up children unto Abraham," or, "turn these stones into bread." He can so easily turn five loaves of bread and two little fishes into around 6 tons of food; or pour from a nearly empty flask, a 100 gallons of oil; or turn a 100 gallons of water into fine wine, the best, the master of the feast said.

When God places His anointing on a ministry, or a servant, then that ministry, or that servant *will be blessed*, whether or not you or I give one cent. Blessing ministries, or feeding the hungry, or clothing the poor, does *not depend* upon you or me. How egotistical of man to suppose that it does.

So then, why the urgency to feed the hungry, clothe the poor, do good and hurt not? Because He knows that giving blesses the giver, as praise and admiration of good things (And God is good, all good) blesses the praiser.

And how much should I give? How much? Indeed, must we ask that question? "Freely you have received, freely give."

"God loves a cheerful giver." "Give and it shall be given unto you..."

But what about tithing? Well, what about it?

"Tithing" is a guide, a letter guide. "All scripture (law and the prophets) is profitable for doctrine, for reproof, for correction, for instruction..," but now we are free. "I will (now) put my laws into their hearts, and in their minds." "If you love me, keep my commandment." "And this is my commandment, that you love..." "Thou shalt love the Lord thy God with all thy heart and with all thy mind, and with all thy soul, and...thy neighbor as thyself. On these two hangs *all* the law, and everything the prophets said." [Author's paraphrase.]

And how much should I give? Certainly we decide *not* by any measure of need, not by any measure of man, not by any measure of letter or law, but only by the measure of the call in our hearts spoken there by the Holy Spirit. Only then can we be free of the "burden" of giving, and find instead, the joy, the freedom of giving. "Seek ye the Truth, and the Truth shall make you free." "I am...the Truth..."

How much should I give? No *man* can answer that question. Only the Holy Spirit, the Spirit of Truth can answer. But as we learn to listen, then again, the "burden" of giving vanishes away, and in its place we find indeed that the Truth has set us free.

Every call to give is a *new* call, and so can only be answered by the Holy Spirit. He may, one time, tell us to give nothing, or another, to give $5, $10, or $20. Or He may say to pledge, on faith, a hundred dollars a month. But dare we suppose that if the Spirit of Truth calls us to such a faith pledge, that He will not honor that faith pledge?

We are free, beloved, we are free.
>Let us *freely* give,
>   and remain free.

February 6, 1986

TO EACH HIS RAINBOW

Today, I looked at a rainbow
and realized that I was the only one
who could see that rainbow.
The way light is refracted, bent,
in those countless millions of prisms,
means that only by looking through my eyes
could anyone else see
        that particular rainbow.

If someone put her head tightly against mine,
she would see a rainbow;
but because she would be looking
from a slightly different angle, she
would have to see a different rainbow.

I wonder, are not people
        like rainbows?
Surely, as we look at one another,
we look from a different level,
a different angle, a different
social, and intellectual, and educational
and emotional perspective.

To each of us, people are not
what they are, but what they appear to be
from our view, our level, our perspective,
our angle.
And so each acquaintance,
                or friend, or lover,
must be uniquely ours.

That's kind of interesting
isn't it.

                                    Honolulu, Hawaii
                                        May 13, 1970

FROM A SAILOR'S LOGBOOK

Check Your Premises.

If your premise is wrong, all of your logic, however logical, will be wrong.

Check your premises; make *certain* that they agree with God's Word. *Then* your logic will be a useful structure, because it rests on a firm and sure foundation.

September 18, 1986

Assertions

An assertion is not a fact. An assertion may state a fact; but an assertion is not a fact.

Many people, even many Christians, get caught in the subtle difference. A person may say, "The sun will rise tomorrow morning." That is an assertion which does state a fact. But the assertion does not make the fact true.

One may say, "The Bible is true." Again, the assertion does not make the Bible true; for, another may assert, with equal conviction, "The Bible is not true." Obviously, that does not make the Bible untrue. The Bible stands by itself; it is true because it is true, not because of any assertions made about it, just as the sun will rise tomorrow morning no matter what is said about it.

Karl Marx once said, "Tell a man something often enough, and long enough, and eventually he will believe it." That was built on a fundamental of atheistic Communism, called Dialectical Materialism. And built into that is their definition of "truth." Truth is what the Party asserts it is. They really mean that and believe that. And of course, that gives the Party Leaders essentially the power of God over the members.

Many fine, well-meaning women got caught in the web of Feminism because they heard assertions stated with such great conviction, that they took them as facts. But it took an unnecessary number of years before most realized that the assertions had no foundation of truth, or at best, were distortions of the truth. The National Organization For Women has lost around 80 percent of its one-time membership, many joining such groups as Concerned Women for America, because C.W.A.'s assertions are based on the Bible, *the* foundation of truth.

The N.O.W., for awhile, even sponsored classes in "Assertiveness." But, "Though I speak with the toungues of men and of angels, and have not love (truth), I am [nothing]." Many, many women have been deeply hurt by the lie of assertiveness.

During the recent struggle over the City of Roseburg, Oregon's attempt to mandate "health care" by fluoridating our water supply, most of the statements made by the proponents, even by the two medical men, who, as scientists, should have known better, were mere assertions. There was no supporting evidence. They just made assertions with great, apparent conviction.

But, an assertion is not a fact. Thank God, we are learning to discern the difference.

September 18, 1986

Attention

God wants our attention. He would rather give us good things, and will, as long as we give Him our whole attention. But, He *will* have our full attention.

"Thou shalt love the Lord thy God with *all* thy heart, and with *all* thy soul, and with *all* thy strength, and with *all* thy mind...."

September 19, 1986

Blessing

We don't *tell* God how to bless us. We don't even tell our people how to bless themselves. We tell our people how to *give, and God* will bless them.

May 9, 1986

Communication

All communication works on a carrier. The carrier is then modulated to change, in a way, its shape; that is, its pitch, its volume, its character, its quality, yes, its color, if we may.

We are most familiar with voice communication. First, we make a sound, a noise, in our voice box; and then we "shape" the sound, the carrier, with our mouths, tongues, lips and teeth. We modulate the carrier.

The carrier in a telephone line is an electric current. It too, is modulated by a transmitter, which converts the voice, air vibrations to electrical "vibrations" or modulations of the electric current. The receiver then re-converts the modulated carrier back to air, sound waves, which we hear as voice.

Radio works in much the same way, except that the voltages and frequencies are very different. But without a carrier, there would be no radio communication.

Fibre Optics is one of the most exciting communication technologies of our times. The carrier is a beam of light traveling along a tiny fibre of very clear glass. Though not necessarily so in actual practice, in principle it is a simple matter to modulate that beam of light to carry, in converted form, the vibrations of our spoken words. But again, without that beam of light, that carrier, there would be no communication.

But the deep, underlying carrier of all communication is emotion, which always speaks truth; it cannot lie. And there are only two catagories; one is love, the other is hate. I will not here go into all the variations of each category; your own mind can do that for you. But just consider these two carriers.

In the grand, old days of telegraphy, long experienced operators could immediately recognize a colleague's "fist," as readily as we recognize a friend's voice. They even got so they could tell his emotion at the time; "What are you mad about, John?" one would ask.

And in our daily communication with one another, that emotional carrier flows, whether or not we recognize it, or even no matter how hard we may try to mask it.

Oh, con artists, certain kinds of salesmen, some politicians, may occasionally succeed in masking the true carrier of hate (lie, deception, ulterior motive) but only because we are not really listening with our spiritual ears.

But the crucial, crucial point of this whole story is not how, or what we hear. It is how we transmit our communication. What carrier are *we* using, love, or hate. When the carrier is one of the forms of hate, even a mild deception, a seemingly innocuous white lie, the most eloquent presentation will eventually do damage of some kind; it will eventually fail. Marriages, friendships have, over long years sometimes, been lost because one or both thought that they were "getting away with" the masked use of the wrong carrier.

But when the carrier is love, God's love, the most stumbling speech, the most inept writing, the crudest gestures will convey their message of truth, because truth and love indeed are one.

Love, beloved, love. Let your carrier always be love. Even when you must, or feel you must, speak harshly to another, be sure your emotional carrier is switched to Love; and then you can do no harm, for:

"*Love* never faileth..."

September 19, 1986

The Infinite Power of Unity

"Be you one, as my Father and I are One."

Jesus here gave us a principle that is both so simple, and yet so profound, that most of us just pass it by. "Nothing can be that simple," we say; or, "It is absolutely beyond me how *this* group can really work together."

Poignantly aware of this admittedly difficult, but *not* impossible principle, Communists have built a comparatively, numerically small cadre of members that are devastating the world. Occasionally, around the world, in the Diplomatic Corps, business operations, and such, Christians have found themselves having to work closely with dedicated Communists. In some cases, friendships have developed. It is reported that, in confidence, Communists have told their Christian friends, "If you Christians were 10 percent as united as we Communists are, you'd blow us away. But you are so busy fighting each other, we can just slip in and 'cut your tent ropes,' almost at will."

Anyone who watches the White House, and the Halls of Congress, can readily see that, if Tip O'Neil and Ronald Reagan would agree—and they do, much more often than most realize—there is almost nothing, or no one, who could stop them.

But what are some other examples of the focused power of unity? The Laser Beam, electronically focused radiant energy, although still far short of its potential, is a good example. The soft and diffused light now falling upon this page, if, together with the light energy in the rest of the building you are in, if altogether were focused into a single beam one one-hundredth of a micron wide, it could easily cut this page, and the table as well, into two pieces. This would not so much be an exercise of brute power, as of unity.

Years ago, I was in the Zeise Manufacturing Plant in Oberkoken, Germany. In a demonstration of the precision used in building those marvelous, optical instruments, I was handed a small fitting, about the size of a cup, and also a 2- or 3-inch rod, about one-quarter inch in diameter. There was a hole in the fitting.

I was told that the rod would slip into the hole. I tried, carefully, and also with much force, but the rod would not enter. Obviously it was close, but it would not enter. So I handed the assembly back to our guide. With gentle, practiced care, he slipped the rod into the hole. "The precision of the machining is so perfect;" he said, "The clearances so minimal, that the two must be perfectly aligned, or, as you found, the rod will not enter."

The "rapier thrust," so popular in fiction stories of sword fighting days, tells us of the incredible power of unity, when the body, the legs, the arm, the motion of the swordsman, are all at one in pressing that thin, sharp, two edged instrument into one point on the body of his opponent.

A "Truism," falsely so called, as they often are, says, "Sticks and stones may break my bones, but words can never harm me." The writer of that "catchy" saying had never read Hebrews, Chapter 4, verse 12, "For the word of God is living, and powerful, and sharper than any two-edged sword, piercing even to the dividing asunder of soul and spirit, *and* of the joints and marrow..."

It is not the bludgeoning, bulldozing power of the Word of God that does the work. It is the perfectly focused, perfectly machined, perfectly coordinated unity, the absolute oneness of the Word of God that pierces the most formidable defenses against its infinite truth. And this applies in the physical, political, economic, material world as well. "Not by might, nor by power, but by My Spirit, saith the Lord of Hosts."

Oh that Christians will draw from the Word of God, what it really means, and demonstrates by the command, "Be you one, as My Father and I are One."

September 20, 1986

Too Much Credit

We give the Adversary altogether too much credit. Christians have ridiculed Flip Wilson for his "funny" remark, "The Devil made me do it." And then Christians, in effect, say the same thing.

So let us study this phenomenom just a bit. First, if Satan *cannot* make a Born-Again Christian sick or poor, then we must conclude that those "afflictions" come either from God, or man—or both. And, since our Father is indeed Sovereign in this Universe, it would have to follow that, even if He does not directly "cause" our affliction—and there are hundreds of Scriptures where He does—He most certainly allows it to happen. And, according to the Bible, to allow something to happen that "it is in thy power to prevent," is the same as doing it. Our Father *is* in control.

But second, if Satan *can* make a Born-Again Christian sick or poor, it would be axiomatic that he can make us healthy and/or wealthy.

I think that most Christians would agree that the Adversary's primary objective is to draw us away from God. Taking that as our premise then, must we not conclude that his best tool would be health or wealth, not sickness or poverty?

We give him altogether too much credit. The Devil is *not* the opposite of God. There is no opposite of God. He is Sovereign in this Universe. He *is* God, and *He* alone.

April 1992

More Spiritual? — Or Less

Prophesy, like poetry, is, to some degree at least, emotion driven. And worship is, of course, an emotional expression. But, losing emotional control, as far too often happens, is not necessarily being *more* Spiritual.

And in this context, is it not written? "And the spirits of the prophets are subject to the prophets. For God is not the Author of confusion, but of peace..."

1 Cor. 14:32-33

April 1992

"TREASURE IN EARTHEN VESSELS" II

A beautiful Brother, David Owen, said something to me in Church one night about what happens as we grow in the Lord. His simple statement was yet so profound, it ignited the following prophesy:

"As we grow in the Lord, we are able, or allowed, to see more of the 'treasure' in each other. But as we are given the capability, and the authority, to see more of the 'treasure,' then it *must* follow, we will see more of the 'earthen vessel.'"

"Of course, as we see more of the 'earthen vessel,' we *must*, absolutely must utilize the gift of grace that commands, and enables us to tolerate those so earthly flaws that are, by nature, in that 'earthen vessel.'"

What a marvelous plan, what a *marvelous* plan.

October 26, 1986

For Ramona:

THE REST OF GOD

Could I now take the time
>to write a poem to my love?
And if I did; what would it be, a song of seas
>and storms, and stars above?

Or would it be a song of inner peace,
>of quiet confidence, of rest
in Him,
and in the gift He gives, of wife,
and counselor, and friend, who bids me cease
from paradox of *striving* for
the peace He says is mine?

I really think the very best
is doing what her wise and loving counsel says,
of letting go, of letting God,
and living, fully truly, freely
>in *His* rest.

>>>March 31, 1986

For Ramona:

THE WRITTEN WORD

"A note," she said,
"Write me a simple note,
and then I'll know;
"I'll read the lovely words,
   'I love you,'
e'en though the spelling says no more
than just, 'hello.'"

"The spoken words, how sweet the flow,
and words of song, they fill me so.
But when they're written
   in a simple note,
I read, 'I love you,'
e'en though the spelling says no more
than just, 'hello.'"

          October 2, 1987

For Pastors everywhere:

THE LONELINESS OF COMMAND

"Does anyone really care," he asked.
And I just stood there, dumb.
"Can he not see? Does he not know?"
And yet my lips were numb.

"But have *you* told him, child of Mine?
Have *you* touched him with *your* hand?
Have *you* looked into his tired eyes,
and said, 'I understand.'?"

I asked a precious Sister
to share a prayer with me,
that God would tell our Captain
of his great worth—that we,
and all the flock he shepherds
truly value such as he.

And she answered with a lovely smile,
and said, "He knows we care."
And again that Voice of Thunder told,
that life is more than prayer,
"But have *you* told him, child of Mine?
Have *you* touched him with *your* hand?

Have *you* looked into his tired eyes,
and said, 'I understand.'?"

And then we changed our prayer and cried,
"Forgive us Lord, we pray;
seal off our lazy lips that lied;
move *us* to *act—this day.*"
Matt. 25:34-46

July 1991.

THE QUESTION

One day, not so very long ago, a beautiful lady was seeking her own ministry, "Lord, give *me* a ministry. My husband has a ministry; but I am intelligent, capable, willing; Lord, give *me* a ministry."

And the Lord gave her His answer, "Look across the table, across the room; see that man, the husband I have given you? There, is your ministry."

And wisdom gripped her as the revelation flooded her heart and mind. "Of course, my husband, God's man; *there is my ministry*, could any woman, any real woman, ask for a greater ministry?"

When I heard that story, my mind rushed back to a question a young Bible School Student asked his teacher at Abbott Loop Bible School in Anchorage, Alaska. He was 24 years old, married, with one child. He would soon be graduating, and leaving to Pastor a new church.

And this was his question, obviously paraphrased, but, his question: "How do we men inspire our women to use their intimate knowledge of their men's weak points, their knowledge of the secret (and sometimes not so secret) chinks in his armor, not as her secret weapon with which to control, or limit, or restrict him, but rather as points to protect, or defend, so that he, with her as his rearguard and support can then be the whole person, the undefeatable man God designed 'them' to be?"

"So God created man in His own *imaqe*, in the image of God created He him, male and female created He them." Gen. 1:27

"And they two shall be one flesh; so then they are no more two, but one flesh." Mark 10:8

"In quietness and in confidence shall be your strength." Isa. 30:15.

Yet no man can be quiet, confident, or strong, if he has, as too many men have, a wife that he has failed to inspire to cover with her heart, her mind, even her very life, the chinks that are in the armor of every man.

September, 1986

FORWARD TO "GOD'S FAMILY ORDER"

Wrapped thoroughly within the context of the following collection of Scriptures, are four vital premises: (1.) Woman was made for man, not man for woman; (2.) Wives are to submit to husbands, not husbands to wives; (3.) Wives are to adapt themselves to their husbands, not husbands to their wives; and (4.) In the context of the family order, not before God of course, but in the context of the family structure and order, women are secondary to men, not men secondary to women.

God has an order. And until men demand that God's order prevail in marriages, *and*, women submit to that order, there will *never* be the harmony in marriages that our God has clearly ordained; the Feminist (Satanic) agenda of discord and conflict will prevail. And all counseling, all our efforts, our worldly efforts to achieve harmony, will continue to be no more than "...tinkling cymbals, or sounding brass...."

Dean Nichols
January 1993

GOD'S FAMILY ORDER

Matt 10:36 (King James Bible)—"Think not that I am come to send peace on the earth; I came not to send peace, but a sword. For I am come to set a man at variance against his father, and the daughter against her mother, and the daughter-in-law against her mother-in-law. And a man's foes shall be they of his own household."

Gen. 2:18 (Living Bible)—"And the Lord God said, 'It isn't good for man to be alone; I will make a companion for him, a helper suited to his needs.'"

Gen. 3:16 (Amplified Bible)—"To the woman He said, 'I will greatly multiply your grief and your suffering in pregnancy and the pangs of child-bearing; with spasms of distress you shall bring forth children; yet your desire and craving shall be for your husband, and he shall rule over you.'"

1 Cor. 11:3 (Amplified Bible)—"But I want you to know and realize that Christ is the head of every man, the head of a woman is her husband, and the Head of Christ is God."

1 Cor. 11:7-9 (Amplified Bible)—"For a man ought not to wear anything on his head [in church], for he is the image and [reflected] glory of God, [that is, his function of government reflects the majesty of

the divine rule]; but woman is [the expression of] man's glory (majesty, pre-eminence).

"For man was not [created] from woman, but woman from man; neither was man created on account of or for the benefit of woman, but woman on account of and for the benefit of man."

1 Cor. 14:34-37 (Living Bible)—"Women should be silent during the church meetings. They are not to take part in the discussion, for they are subordinate to men as the Scriptures also declare. If they have any questions to ask, let them ask their husbands at home, for it is improper for women to express their opinions in church meetings.

"You disagree? And do you think that the knowledge of God's will begins and ends with you Corinthians? Well, you are mistaken! You who claim to have the gift of prophecy or any other special ability from the Holy Spirit should be the first to realize that what I am saying is a commandment from the Lord himself."

Eph. 5:22-24 (NIV)—"Wives, submit to your husbands as to the Lord. For the husband is the head of the wife as Christ is the head of the church, his body, of which he is the Savior. Now as the church submits to Christ, so also wives should submit to their husbands in everything."

Eph. 5:33 (Amplified Bible)—"However, let each man of you (without exception) love his wife as [being in a sense] his very own self; and let the wife see that she respects and reverences her husband— that she notices him, regards him, honors him, prefers him, venerates and esteems him; and that she defers to him, praises him, and loves and admires him exceedingly."

Col. 3:18 (Amplified Bible)—"Wives, be subject to your husbands—subordinate and adapt yourselves to them - as is right and fitting and your proper duty in the Lord."

1 Tim. 2:11-14 (Amplified Bible)—"Let a woman learn in quietness in entire submissiveness. I allow no woman to teach or to have authority over men; she is to remain in quietness and keep silence [in religious assemblies]. For Adam was first formed, then Eve; and it was not Adam who was deceived, but [the] woman who was deceived and deluded and fell into transgression."

Titus 2:3-5 (Living Bible)—"Teach the older women to be quiet and respectful in everything they do. They must not go around speaking evil of others and must not be heavy drinkers, but they should be teachers of goodness. These older women must train the younger women to live quietly, to love their husbands and their children, and to be sensible and clean minded, spending their time in their own homes, being kind and obedient to their husbands, so that the Christian faith can't be spoken against by those who know them."

1 Pet. 3:1-6 (Amplified Bible)—"In like manner you married women, be submissive to your own husbands—subordinate yourselves as being secondary to and dependent on them, and adapt yourselves to them. So that even if any do not obey the Word [of God], they may be won over not by discussion but by the [godly] lives of their wives, when they observe the pure and modest way in which you conduct your-

selves, together with your reverence [for your husband. That is, you are to feel for him all that reverence includes]—to respect, defer to, revere him [revere means] to honor, esteem (appreciate, prize), and [in the human sense] adore him; [and adore means] to admire, praise, be devoted to, deeply love and enjoy [your husband].

"Let not yours be the [merely] external adorning with [elaborate] interweaving and knotting of the hair, the wearing of jewelry, or changes of clothes; but let it be the inward adorning and beauty of the hidden person of the heart, with the incorruptible and unfading charm of a gentle and peaceful spirit, which (is not anxious or wrought up, but) is very precious in the sight of God.

"For it was thus that the pious women of old who hoped in God were (accustomed) to beautify themselves, and were submissive to their husbands—adapting themselves to them as themselves secondary and dependent upon them. It was thus that Sarah obeyed Abraham (following his guidance and acknowledging his headship over her by) calling him lord—master, leader, authority. And you are now her true daughters if you do right..."

September 17, 1990

THE RATIO

Many years ago, my cousin Frank, and our mutual uncle, Jim, were digging sugar beets in the Yakima Valley. These were farmers, earthy. Neither had yet committed his life to the Lord Jesus Christ.

But, though they were men of the earth, articulate in the rhetoric of the earth, they were also brilliant minds, thoughtful men, inquiring minds. The machine they were operating together had probably been designed by those minds, and built by those skilled hands.

Years later we laughed at how their conversation must have sounded to one listening from a 1000 feet away. To hear each other, they were, of necessity, shouting above the immediate roar of the machine. "Frank, I don't think God would... Watch that _____ __ __ _____." "Oh_____, I busted that one all to ___." "Yeah, well, I don't think God would...."

An incongruous conversation? Yes, but it also proves my point, as we shall later see.

They were discussing the meaning, the balances of life.

"I don't think God is really concerned about most of *what* we do;" Uncle Jim continued, "In fact, I think we can say that life is 90 percent filler (Of course he used a much more earthy word than filler, but he really meant filler.), and 10 percent serious. Now those numbers might not be precise, but you get the point.

"But using those numbers, let's look more closely at what happens when we alter that ratio, even a little bit. First, that 90 percent filler is 100 percent filler. But that makes the 10 percent serious, 100 percent serious. So, a shift of only 1 percent, though it won't affect the filler much at all, wreaks havoc with the serious. A 10 percent, or worse, a 20 percent shift in the serious can make of one, a worthless playboy, and of another, an overcharged zealot."

But back to these men's language. Yes, I know the scripture that says to let no corrupt communication come out of your mouth. But that is a charge to one who has heard, and accepted, and committed. The communication from *his* mouth is meant now to be shifted from the filler, to the serious.

Just a year or two ago, a strident Feminist surrendered to the Lord. She knew, and was fluent in every obscene, profane, blasphemous word in the book. She also had a brilliant mind, an observant mind; she knew that she was in trouble. So she looked up to heaven and, using that eloquent vocabulary to its fullest, said, in effect, "OK, I give up; do your thing." The evidence is overwhelming that our loving, forgiving, glorious Father never heard the corrupt words spewing from her mouth. He heard only the cry of a penitent heart, and He saved her from the Hell toward which she was bound, and swept her into His Kingdom. Today, she is a loving, strong, zealous soldier in the Army of our

Lord. She has her ratio of filler and serious in balance now.

Oh, we need the filler in our day to day living. If we poured the essential elements of fertilizer onto the roots of a plant, with no filler, no dilution at all, we'd burn the plant to death in hours. The diffused light, falling upon this page, and making reading possible, if it were focused into a laser beam and directed into your eyes, it would burn them out of their sockets.

Even Jesus came to us in the form of man so that the infinite brilliance and force of God's power would not blow us away. He walked, and rested, and dined, and fellowshipped with people, and delighted in such beautiful things as flowers and children. He even told a fisherman how better to catch fish. He understood the ratio very well.

Too many Christians are far too serious. Hang loose, let go, let God. And too many Christians are spending far too much time, and, too much money on the filler. Are you, flippant Christian, any better than the infidel?

But you, unbeliever, if you are 91:9, or worse, 95:5, you are in deep trouble. Yes, the 85:15, incredibly overzealous Christian, is wasting a lot of time, a lot of living, a lot of energy in his zeal; but, he is still living. You, unbeliever, are dying. And that, *is* serious.

October 22, 1986

"...THEY *TWO* SHALL BE *ONE*..."

"For this cause shall a man leave Father and Mother, and shall cleave to his wife, and they two shall be one flesh."

Doctors, and Nurses, and Pastors *must* understand that there is a *terrible* rending, far, far more devastating when one loses a lifelong mate than that which occurs with any other loss. Oh, we all have to deal, now and then, with those who are hurting from such a loss; but the above three are the front line soldiers, the officers, who must also guide the rest of us through this storm.

I am not talking, in this paper, of divorce. Surely there is unfinished hurt in divorce that often takes much longer to heal. And some of the things we learn here, can be applied to the loss in divorce. And I am not talking here about short-term marriages. Although who would deny the searing pain when young love, young hopes and dreams are brought crashing down by the death of a young husband or wife.

I am talking here of the unique, the very special rending that occurs when a lifetime marriage, 30 or 40 years or more, is torn by the death of a mate.

A marriage is not meant to be a partnership, or even a friendship; although of course, they should be good friends. But God's Word says that they are to become one, a relationship unique and so special that there is *no other* relationship like it.

In Ecclesiastes 4:12 we read that, "A threefold cord is not quickly broken." And that is true of marriage. The weaving of the fibres of strength that each brings into one cord does indeed make for a oneness much stronger than the sum of the threads. But this can apply to other relationships as well.

Laminated wood, where thinner boards are bonded together to become a single, large beam, again produces a structure stronger than the sum of the parts, because they lend strength to each other, and so are multiplied. But this is done by the hand of man. So much depends on the bonding material, its quality, and life.

Much closer to marriage, is the steel fencing sword of medieval times. Metallurgists today, still do not know how they produced such fine steel, but they do know how they fabricated those incredibly flexible, thin strong blades.

A rod was cast, perhaps an inch or so in diameter. Heated red hot, it was pounded out into a long ribbon, twice the length desired. Heated again, it was folded back upon itself, and pounded out again. When red hot steel is pounded upon red hot steel, it welds together. (In fact, before we had gas or electric arc welding that was the only way we knew of welding.) This folding and hammering process was repeated again and again, and the process developed, not only a lamination but also a grain in the steel much like the grain in wood, with the extra strength along the grain that wood has.

When the artisan was satisfied, he ground the sword to its final shape and edge, tempered the metal, fashioned a hilt, and presented to the swordsman, a single blade of steel, tough, resilient, strong, with a strength far beyond the bar that had first been cast.

Oh, these are all much like marriage, threads woven together, pulling together; beams bonded to one another, lending strength to one another; ribbons of steel heated and hammered till they become one blade, tough and resilient and lasting. But even the single blade, can be determined to be the welding together of many layers of steel.

Only a tree, with its many roots, its many branches, but its *single* trunk can be likened to a marriage. "...the two shall be one..."

So let us look at a tree to learn what happens when a lifetime marriage is torn in half by death.

The roots spread out in all directions, gripping the ground, feeding upon the earth, holding the tree erect in the face of every storm, whether from the north or south.

The trunk is the one, single marriage, not two, but one.

And let the branches, limbs, and twigs represent members of the family, and friends, bonded through long years.

Once in a while, a twig is broken off, and the loss is noted, a card may be received, and appreciated.

Less often, a branch is lost, a funeral is attended, pain is felt. But soon, the other branches fill in, leaving only a small scar.

And then, sometimes, a major limb is torn away, as when a beautiful, vibrantly alive, 24-year-old son, is swept into the sea, giving his breath of life to the unforgiving sea. The tree is somewhat out of balance now; there is a gaping wound, there is much bleeding. Healing takes a long, long time. Always the tree will be marked by the scar from that tearing. But the tree is still one tree. Healing does come, slowly, but it comes.

But when a lifetime mate is lost, half the tree, half of that single trunk, half the roots are torn away. If it is the north half that is gone, then there is no longer support against the north winds; the tree fights to stand, with only its southern roots to grip the ground. The northern cold now penetrates to its very heart. The tree cries out for help to stem the gushing flood from that open, gaping wound. It cries for help to stand, just to stand, when the north winds blow.

And then the wind turns to the south. Friends do not notice the change. Winds change. But they do notice that now the tree is standing, strong, able. "Good old George, I knew he'd come through." And so they drift away, called by the never ending demands on their own lives.

But the wind changes again. A gale from the north. And the tree, fighting alone now, for its very life, cries out for help. It had grown a few new roots to the north, while the south wind blew, but it still cries for help.

And only a very few, a very special few, come with help; because, somehow, only a very special few know that this was not the loss of a twig, or a branch, or a limb. Half the tree is gone.

October 24, 1986

"...I'LL GIVE YOU GOLD"

Poems have been written,
and stories often told
of the emptiness of houses,
how their warmth has turned to cold.

So then it makes one wonder
what that warmth consisted of.
Was it the structure of the building;
or was it comradship and love?

What was it filled the hallways?
What made the rooms aglow
with the Spirit of His presence?
Can we ever really know?

Yes,
for where two or three are gathered
in the Name of Christ our Lord,
there will His Spirit linger
bringing peace and sweet accord.

But for now my house seems empty,
and though it's never really cold,
and His love is ours for sharing,
still, the distance has its hold.

Oh the distant bells are ringing,
but they are bells of iron and brass;
we see our love still blooming,
but as through a clouded glass.

I miss your warming presence,
your footsteps and your voice,
that put substance to our sharing,
and make my heart rejoice.

For,
though the storms have torn upon us,
and the years their story told,
we've known tarnished brass and iron,
the emptiness and cold;

Still the filling Savior promised,
with His warming words of old,
"For your iron I'll give you silver;
for your brass I'll give you gold."

March 17, 1980

CONTRASTS

"The whole earth be filled with His glory." And it is; yet intermixed is contamination and death; the bacteria for decay and rot.

I am not a horticulturist; but after nearly 70 years, one learns much. And a profound lesson? Living things don't rot.

Well, look at your fruit trees and garden. Take a bright, new board, fresh from the lumber yard. Plant it in the "rich" soil of your orchard beside the root of a tree. In a year, dig up the wooden board, and, look at the wooden root of the tree. Both of wood, but the board has rotted away; the living root has grown; and both in the same soil.

A melon, or squash, or tomato, detached from the vine, its source of life, and lying on that "rich" soil of the same garden that gives life to the vines, will quickly decay and rot, while others, lying on the ground but still receiving life from the vine, will not.

And what is the lesson here? Somewhere it is written, "You cannot really call a man good, if he is totally denied the opportunity to be bad." Jesus said, in *His* prayer for us, "I'm not asking You (Father God) to take them out of the world (garden), but to keep them safe from Satan's power (contamination, decay, death.)" And in the words of Joshua, "*Choose* you this day whom you will serve." We have a choice; we must make a choice. That is; if we do nothing, we *have* death, but if we *choose* Jesus, we have life. "He that believes on Him is not condemned, but he that believes not is *condemned* already." And in Deuteronomy Chapter 30, Verse 19, Moses speaks, "Oh that you would choose life, that you and your children might live."

Contrasts; life *is* contrasts. The natural state of the universe is darkness. Only when there is brilliant sunlight do shadows show up, dark and sharp in outline; the warmth and coziness of a fire is best felt when there is a snowstorm outside; comfort and solace is most appreciated when we are recovering from deep grief; and oh the joy of good food when we are hungry. Gravity holds us down, and makes our load heavy; but working against that gravity, we build strength. A flower garden is lovely, yes, but are flowers more beautiful than when seen blooming in the desert?

We all are very "earthen vessels;" but where did Jesus place the treasure of His love? "...we have this treasure in earthen vessels that the excellency of the power may be [seen as] of God and not of us."

Cling to Jesus, the Vine, the source of life; and then "...glory in tribulation...knowing *that*" for we who *live*, the bacteria for decay and death that permeate this garden we call the earth, can produce for us, only growth, the glory of life, the display of *His* treasure, because He meant for it to be seen in the sharp contrast to the darkness of this "earthen vessel."

Contrasts: Death, stagnation, and darkness, or, life, and growth, and glory. "Choose you this day whom you will serve."

October 22, 1986

THE PERFECT MARRIAGE

"Well, if a man loved a woman like *that*, she would have no problem at all in submitting to him."

My sister-in-law is an angel. Well, to be more earthly, she is a very mortal woman. But she stood by me during the worst storm of my life; and she did so in such a quiet way that, perhaps, no one else saw or felt the strength she fed into my bleeding soul. When she was close, I *knew* God was close; I wasn't so terribly, terribly alone.

Still, she is a North Dakota, Norwegian Farm girl, who has known her own storms. But to survive on those North Dakota farms, one had to be tough, even hard, to some degree. And "anyone knows," those Norwegians are certainly not noted for being pussy willows.

So I knew that I had struck gold. The blade of truth I had just thrust had pierced to her very heart, and, because she is truly God's child, the exposed truth in that heart was at once one with the truth of God. The full depth of that quotation from the Bible that I had just spoken had found a resonant chord in her. Truth always rings with truth.

We were alone in her living room, watching time turn the twilight shadows into night. We were discussing marriage. We agreed that, in most cases, sadly, marriages are lived in some kind of conflict, some kind of struggle, or at least competition. And we agreed that it *should not be so.*

"Well Sis," I was saying, "It used to be that we could operate our marriages on the consensus of public opinion. The social fabric told us what to do; and that worked quite well because that consensus was itself built on the Word of God.

"The Puritans, and the many other Christian groups who dominated our early culture, our schools, our politics, and our media, held those institutions, whether they knew it or not, in the context of Christian principles. And so, our marriages were guided by those principles, principles that worked, because they were of God.

"But now, after just a few decades of cooling by the Church, Humanism has grasped onto man's innate need for some moral base, and has given him, through those same institutions a moral base, but, in perverted form. The statement, 'It is more blessed to give than to receive,' is not logical, and so it was discarded for the much more logical principle, 'Take care of number one; if you don't take care of yourself, who will?'

"The Humanist perversion, with its destructive logic, has even led most 'good' marriages, even most Christian marriages into a perverted form of 'rule and submit.' Most marriages operate now on a dominate/buckle-under ratio. Often this appears to work quite well, so often that others call this one or that one a 'good' marriage. Rarely, the husband dominates 100% of the time; but in the above 'good' marriages it is more apt to be in the ratio of 90-10 to 60-40; that is, the husband dominates the larger percentage of time, and the wife buckles under. And the wife dominates the smaller percentage of time, and the husband buckles under. It is often called just give and take, because the conflict appears gentle; but *conflict* it is. Even if one only asserts, or worse, manipulates, the other gives up, or buckles under.

"One grand, old farmer even told me just the other day, that he always operated under the rule, 'Outside, I'm boss; inside, she's boss.' A clear case of simply trading dominance periods. They are retired now, 90 percent of their time is spent 'inside.' Yes, the marriage still 'works,' but *none of this* is according to God's Word.

"You know, Sis," I continued, "Those of us who are not only deeply concerned for marriage, but who also must believe that God's principles were designed to work, we must return to the source, to God's Word, as He meant for it to be read, and followed. We both know that, according to His Word, the husband is supposed to 'rule his household.' But that word 'rule,' as used in this way, clearly implies consent of the governed."

I then quoted to her the scripture that has been used by so many Feminists to stir up the Spirit of rebellion in the women of this world: "Wives, submit yourselves unto your own husbands, *as* unto the Lord." Even though I emphasized that crucial, two-letter word 'as,' still, the silence deepened across that darkened room. My angel sister does not talk much, but I noted the subtle deepening of the silence.

But then the Holy Spirit *must* have spoken through my mortal voice when I said, "Just as most Christians, and certainly all Feminists miss the full depth of that above scripture, because they miss that two-letter word on which it turns, so they miss the other half of this great principle of God, 'Husbands, love your wives *as* Christ also loved the Church, *and* gave Himself for her.'"

There was the loveliness, the richness of pure gold when she spoke, "Well, if a man loved a woman like *that*, she would have no problem at all in submitting to him." I knew indeed, I had struck gold.

We have some work to do, fellow Christians; we have some housecleaning to do. The "logical" principles of Humanism must go; *but*, as they are discarded, we *must* immediately replace them with God's principles, clearly understood.

The whole garment of society is made from the fabric of families. And the only thing that can keep the family from unraveling, is the border binding bond of a perfect marriage.

"Wives, submit *as*..." "Husbands, love *as*..."

February 1987

NOVEMBER 10, 1989

My Beloved Wife, AKA Swede, Dakota, Ramona,

I missed going to the store and picking out a "storebought" card for this, our fifth year together. I have apologized, and been forgiven. Still, I want to make up for it in some way. So how about this:

At our latitude, it is about twenty thousand miles around the earth. So every day, we travel twenty thousand miles together. But that is *one* day. In one year, we travel three hundred and sixty-five times that, or seven million, three hundred thousand miles together. But still that isn't all. In the five years we have been married, we have travelled five times that together, or thirty-six million, five hundred thousand miles, side by side.

And still that isn't all. It is some over ninety-seven million miles to the sun, depending on apogee, or perigee. The sun is only some less than one million miles in diameter. That makes the diameter of the earth's orbit around the sun to be nearly two hundred million miles. Its circumference then, or the distance the earth travels in one year, to be around six hundred million miles. And that, times five years, is three billion miles. And none of this even considers the incredible distance our solar system has travelled in our galaxy during this time, nor the distance our galaxy has travelled through space.

But even the calculations above mean that we have travelled together, during these five years, a total of over, well over, three billion, thirty-six million, five hundred thousand miles. And that is a long, long way for two to travel together.

So here, I say, here, my love, here is to at least another fifteen billion miles together, plus or minus a few million miles; but all of them miles together.

      Happy Fifth Anniversary,
      Dean

TO TITHE OR NOT TO TITHE...

We were in Abbott Loop Christian Center in Anchorage, Alaska. The 2000-seat auditorium was nearly full. A tall, gangly Missionary to Africa was there, presenting his work to this Congregation.

A man in his 40s, he was a very poor speaker. Although I could tell that he himself was keenly interested in his work, and it was considerable, there surely was no dynamic speaker, holding our attention this night.

He told of their work there, and then presented a few reels of 8-millimeter movie (in a 2000-seat auditorium), of his work, adding some commentary. Then he preached for us. I could not say that his preaching was pathetic, but eloquent preaching was *not* his calling.

Later in the Service, a collection, rare at Abbott Loop, was taken for this man's work in Africa. A number of Kentucky Fried Chicken buckets were set on chairs near the platform. Singing began, as the people walked forward with their offerings.

As had developed my custom, I had started through the numbers in my mind, seeking the Holy Spirit's direction on how much if any, *I* should give. Zero, $5— $10— $15— $20. Usually, I settled somewhere between zero and $20, and more commonly between $10 and $15. But this night, the numbers kept going,— $40— $50— $60— $70. "Lord," I cried in my mind, "This man's presentation was crude, his movie was incredibly amateurish, his preaching was most unpolished, to put it kindly."

Well, I *had* gotten some resistance at $70, so I backed back down— $60— $50— $40— $30. But again the resistance, came; so I started back up. The only number that gave me peace, was $50. "Lord," I almost gasped, "You want me to give $50?" But the compelling peace remained, so I wrote a check for $50, and took it forward.

Later in the service, as was their custom, an announcement was made on the total amount of the offering. I had known of many $2000 to $3000 offerings for departing Pastors, teams going out to start a new Church somewhere, other visiting Evangelists. But this night the announcement brought forth a soft but audible gasp across even this large body. The amount was $8,500. Clearly, clearly, the Holy Spirit had not spoken to me alone; He had spoken to an entire Congregation.

But the drama was not yet over. Immediately a man, far to my left, stood up and called out, "Pastor, before the collection began, God told me that that man was to receive $10,000 tonight, *and*, that if the collection fell short of that, I was to make up the difference. So my check for $1500 will be in your office tomorrow morning."

Ten thousand dollars; not because the speaker had earned it, not because this Congregation was rich, or even large. It came because a people listened to the Holy Spirit.

But how did my own part in all this come about? Well, it came from God, of course, but it came to me through my daughter, Judy. "Dad," she announced one day on the phone, "I've stopped tithing."

Anyone who knows this precious child of God would know that a drama is about to be played. So I waited.

"OK." I said. "That sounds interesting. Tell me about it."

"Well," she began, "We are under the New Testament, the new Covenant, aren't we; so we are not bound by the old. Isn't that right?"

I conceded the assertion, but countered with the scripture, "'All scripture is profitable for doctrine, for reproof, for correction..,' and that is speaking of the Old Testament."

"Yes," she agreed, "I won't argue with that. But Jesus said He would now write His laws on our hearts, in our minds. He clearly did not mean just the Ten Commandments, or the Mosaic law. He meant, as He said, all the law and all that the Prophets said."

My own thoughts raced, "Yes, '...on these two, the whole law hangeth, and the Prophets.'"

But Judy was rushing on, "He said that the Holy Spirit would be our teacher, our guide. Surely, as with all the other "Law," we can, and should use the principle of tithing as a guideline, a baseline, so to speak. But if we are going to use the wonder of the Spirit of Life that is within each Born-Again Christian, then we must listen to *that* voice, be ultimately responsible to that voice, and none other, whether that voice says to give zero, or 100 percent.

"Of course we must 'assemble ourselves together', of course we must read the Word, of course we must listen to preaching; but the ultimate decision we make, in every instance, *must* be what the Spirit of Life within us tells us to do.

"It is true, that operating under the principle of freedom, places a terrible responsibility on the Christian; it would be so easy to cheat. But, although we are told of this freedom in Galations 5:13, we are also warned. It says, 'For, Brethren, you have been called unto liberty; only use not liberty for an occasion to the flesh (or self), but by love serve (or give to) one another (God's work).' For those who cannot accept that responsibility, then perhaps they should remain under the rigid confines of the Law. But Jesus said we are free."

That was good preaching; but I was still thinking of that entire Old Testament, "But Judy, we can't just throw that Old Testament all out, can we?" I argued.

"Oh no," came her ready answer, "We need all of that. Look, Dad, you understand computers quite well. Think of the Old Testament as a software package, a data base for our 'now' problems. The Law didn't work, because it was too rigid. In today's world it is obvious that a man making $5000 a month might wince at a $500 tithe; but he'd still have $4500 left after he made it. But a man with a family, house and car payments, and three kids to feed, and making $500 a month, just could not tithe $50 a month. But even that analogy breaks down.

"The man with $5000 a month just might have very real expenses that would take every dollar of his income; and the man with $500 a month just might have free rent, no car, or need of one, and more food than he can eat because he works on a truck farm. He might easily be able to tithe $50. You see, the law didn't work, because it was too rigid. That's why I stopped tithing, and started giving."

Light illuminated my mind as she spoke those last three words, "...and started giving." Of course, of course, God loves a cheerful *giver*, not tither; 'Give and it shall be given unto you;' not tithe and it shall be tithed to you.

Intrigued as I was with this radical concept, I still had questions: "OK, how do you decide how much to give?"

"Easy, Dad, we listen to the Holy Spirit. Every call to give *must* be a new call. With the endless stream of factors surrounding a need, *and* our own financial, and emotional, and spiritual status at the time, we must say again that the rigidity of the Law could not possibly cover every factor, or meld them all together. Only the Holy Spirit can do that."

Then she outlined that little numbers game she ran through in her mind at each call to give. The one I had copied at Abbott Loop.

"It makes giving so much more fun, Dad. In fact, let me warn you. If you start practicing this, it will shock you, one day, when you discover how much you are giving. Usually, it is so much that the Holy Spirit doesn't need to call up the tithing data in that data base; but it is there, just in ease. It has its influence on the 'now' decision. But Jesus came to set us free, Dad. I'm free, really free in my giving now."

And that is how I came to give $50 to a Missionary to Africa, one night, and finding myself laughing in my spirit, with my Lord. "Didn't I tell you," He was saying, "That I love a hilarious giver."

Oh, I do find that I must be careful, when searching my mental computer for the Lord's direction, that I do not allow my feelings of the moment to influence my decision. Just as a sense of depression is a poor reason for giving little, so is a sense of euphoria a poor reason to give much. It must, and can be, only the Spirit of God to which I respond.

It has been ten years now, since that dramatic night. I have made many mistakes in giving, in living the freedom He has given me. But I always return to this: The only place where we are bound is in our commitment to Jesus. We are His slaves. Yet even there we are free, free in His blessed captivity. *His* blessed captivity, *not* the letter of the Law. 2 Corinthians 4:6 now leaps off the page with ringing meaning: "Who also hath made us able ministers of the new Testament, not of the letter, but of the Spirit; for the letter killeth, but the Spirit giveth life."

Listen to the Spirit, O Beloved, listen to the Spirit; and if He says to give zero, then, without guilt, give zero. But if you are going to listen to Him when He says to give zero, then you must listen to Him when He says to give 10, 20, 50, or even 100 percent.

Bastendorff Beach, Oregon
January 1988

CHANGE

Change is a world's word. They say, "We must 'change' to fit the times."

Ah, but to be highly skilled, and for one to so neglect that skill that he becomes unskilled; that is change, but it is not good.

One may be radiantly healthy, and become very sick. That is change, but it is not necessarily good.

A man may be wise, yet fall into the ways of the world and become foolish. That is change, but it is not good.

One may be financially stable, but through misfortune, or neglect, become heavily in debt. That is change, but again, it is not necessarily good.

But most crucial of all, men have turned from following Jesus, and turned to following Baal. Indeed, that is change, but it surely is not good.

Jesus is the same yesterday, today, and forever. God says, "I change not."

Yet when we get into trouble, whether it be physical, or Spiritual, too often we Christians say with the world, "We need to change."

NO! We must say, "I shall *return* to God's way, God's will, God's Word."

Surigao City
Philippines
May 15, 1987

Gold Beach, Oregon

October 24, 1984

PSR, RB
U.S. Bank
Oak and Main
Roseburg, Oregon, 97470

Hi,

        The sun is shining;
        the NW tradewinds, warm and comforting,
        sing their soft and soothing sounds.
        And the surf,
        ever washing the gentle sands,
        brings peace and healing to my soul.

        And comforting there,
        in the secret place of my mind,
        your loving presence fills,
        and makes my life complete.

                I love you,

                Dean

A STORY

Once upon a time there was a young couple by the names of Dean and Ramona Nichols.

Dean had a small retirement income of around $850 a month, and Ramona worked for U.S. Bank of Oregon. According to a national organization called "Bank Watch," U.S. Bank is one of the strongest in the nation. But banks are notoriously low wage payers. Nothing even remotely as well as Roseburg Forest Products pays, fellas. Still, they got by. Their house was paid for. (After nearly 70 years, it should be.) They were out of debt. It was just that, like everyone else, they were poignantly aware of the increasing cost of things.

One day, Ramona came in from a trip to Safeway Store. She set four bags down on the table with a thump, and then, in silence, methodically set the items upon the countertop. They didn't take up a lot of room. Then she turned to her husband. (I could almost say, "She turned *on* him." She didn't.) But the words, somewhat inflamed by frustration, did have a bit of edge to them, "Do you know what those four bags of groceries cost? $52." She repeated, "$52 for four bags of groceries."

Dean, whose calculator mind had already determined that to be the approximate cost, said, "Yes, that's about what I'd figured. I guess you just have to accept, in this life, that you pay for what you get."

But this was one time when a husband's agreement was *not* appreciated. He was to have his turn.

A few days later, Dean came in from just having gassed up the big, Chevy Suburban with its 40-gallon tank. "Good Grief, Ramona," he sputtered, "I knew I was nearly out of gas, but $35.60; Good Grief!"

But his wife was standing there with a mock expression of deep concern on her face. Slipping through around the edges was a grin. Still, she held that concerned expression, "Yes, that's terrible," she agreed, "But I guess you just have to accept, in this life, that you pay for what you get."

Dean continued to glower for a few moments longer, and then his sense of humor came to the rescue. The irony caught them both, and they laughed, long and hard.

He caught her in his arms and said, "You know, Swede, (He calls her Swede sometimes, because she is a North Dakota, Swedish farm girl.) You know Swede, why don't we just adopt that as our philosophical rule in life, 'You pay for what you get'?" And she agreed.

The following Saturday, he drove downtown on some errands. He stopped at the Farmer's Coop for an 80-lb bag of fertilizer for the lawn. He winced a bit at the $12 price, especially when he knew it was just to make his beautiful front lawn even more green. It would feed not one soul in a hungry world.

But he rationalized that his neighbors, who often spoke of his beautiful lawn, would appreciate it. And, if you want a beautiful lawn, you fertilize it, even at $12 a bag. Isn't that the rule? "You pay for what you get."

On the way home he stopped for the mail. It was bill time. The electric bill alone was for $74.49. "Ouch," he thought, as he realized that much of that cost was for that clothes dryer that was also wearing out his clothes. "Good Grief," he continued in his thoughts, "When will women realize that all that lint you clean out of that lint trap is clothing that you paid a hundred dollars a pound for?"

But then reason took over. He knew that if she had the time, Ramona herself would love to hang the clothes out on the line where the solar clothes dryer is not only free, it does not wear out clothes, *and*, it makes them smell *so* good.

But time; she just did not have the time. Working 45 to 50 hours a week at a demanding job, many times counseling distraught customers; keeping up her home, caring for her husband, and her parents, Ramona just did not have the energy, or the time. The clothes dryer,—though incredibly expensive, gave her time. "Yeah," he thought, "There it is again, 'You pay for what you get.'"

The next day was Sunday, and as was their custom, they drove to Church. As they turned into the large, firm parking lot, Dean, a typical Christian, thought two things, "They really ought to pave this lot. But still, this is nice; even with all the rain, this lot is firm and dry, and, there is plenty of room."

It was just a bit nippy out, so when they stepped through the door of the old, but very sound building, the warm, electric heat welcomed them. "I wonder who pays that electric bill," he thought, "I understand it runs $500 a month. Hmmm, maybe that's why that shambles of a basement that needs refurbishing, still is not done."

But he dismissed the negative thoughts as friends greeted them. And as they stepped into the crowded auditorium, they were greeted by an accomplished orchestra. A piano, an organ, two violins, two guitars, and a saxophone. The music was rich, full, and stirring. They both had received much already, and the service had not yet started.

And then it began. For over an hour, they became lost in praise and worship of a God Who gives so much, and asks so very little.

The singing subsided; it was time to take the offering, someone said. A slight frown crossed Dean's face. "*Take* an *offering*?" he questioned in his mind. "These Churches always want money. Why don't they be honest and call it like it is, 'offering a taking'?"

As the plate came by, he fumbled for his check book. "No time for that," he thought. Yes, he knew there were three $20 bills in his billfold, but, "I do plan to go to the coast tomorrow. Never know what might come up." The plate passed by; he relaxed. He had noted that Ramona had not dropped anything in either. "But what the heck," he was thinking,

"Obviously, neither do the rest of these people give much. There sure wasn't much in that plate."

The sermon that followed was powerful. It seemed especially prepared for Dean and Ramona. And in a good way.

They were stirred, and lifted, and informed, and inspired. It was on giving; the need for the giver to give. "Yes," the Pastor was thundering, "There are needs all around us..."

Dean thought, "You can say that again, Brother, that basement is a disgrace. And this auditorium should be at least quadrupled in size, the way this congregation is growing."

But the Pastor was continuing, "But giving, as designed by Almighty God, is for the giver. The giver *needs* to give. The one who fails to give, when the Holy Spirit says to give, he is the greatest loser of all." Both Dean and Ramona were thinking that they didn't know when they had gotten so much from a sermon.

Later, as they stepped out into that big parking lot, the wind had stopped, and a brilliant sun greeted them, glinting off the windshields of nearly 100 cars. Again Dean's analytical mind began computing. "You know, Swede," he said, almost with wonder, "There is close to one million dollars worth of cars, just in the parking lot of what I thought was a poor Church." Ramona just grinned and shook her head.

As they were driving out, in their own $12,000 Chevrolet Suburban, and commenting to each other on the service, Dean observed, "You know, I always get a lot out of that Church, but you couldn't pay for what we received today." Ramona agreed.

And then Dean fell very silent. Ramona knew what he was thinking. She always knows what he is thinking. A mile down the road, he spoke, "Ramona, you know our rule, 'You pay for what you get,'?"

"Yes," she answered expectantly.

"That rule, ah, that rule wouldn't apply to that little Church back there ——would it?"

Bastendorff Beach, Oregon
January, 1988

[A number of years ago I was attending the Federal Aviation Agency Academy at Oklahoma City. I had sat down at a teletype machine to practice, and had just let my mind run free. The following is what came forth.]

REALITY

"Well now, let us reason together," saith the Lord. Let us consider the written claims of that Book that tells of God's Creation. Maybe there are errors in it; and then again, if we really study and consider that Book, we would find that it speaks truth with a ringing clarity.

When a man or woman tells you something that you have no proof or evidence of, then you consider it and weigh his presentation of it. Does it ring with truth, or is there an undercurrent of falsehood in it? True, con artists are born every day, and the Bible could be the con artist of all time. But con artists are eventually uncovered. Sometimes it is not until after their death, but they are eventually uncovered. Any book that has withstood the test of observation, and even attack, for as long as the Bible has, that book demands *serious* consideration.

Yes, I know that there are many very learned men and women who have written some very convincing arguments against the Bible as the Word of God, by pointing out "obvious" discrepancies. But when I said above, "Let us consider the written claims of that Book," I did not mean to spend time picking at minor, apparent discrepancies. I meant to consider the basic, fundamental facts of the sinfulness of man, the Diety of Jesus, and the simple yet profound plan of salvation. The Bible explains the reason for living, the identity of man, in a way that loudly and clearly rings of reality and truth.

It is not "just a nice way to go, something that emotional people need." The story it tells is the story of reality, real reality.

Is this earthly life reality? One lifetime is but a flash in eternity. Are food and fun and sex and fine homes and football games and television and causes like the United Nations, are these reality?

Or is the real awareness of the identity of men or women who have hooked themselves into eternity of life rather than death by claiming the promises of the Bible, is that reality?

I am 56 years old. Even if I did not start to consider life and just what reality is until I was six years old, it is clear that I have had half a century to consider this mystery. And I have considered it from both sides of the question. Whether I appear now as a "good guy" or not, I can honestly confess that I have known, in intimate detail, the sordid, the beautiful, the thrilling, the exciting, the sensual, the ugly, in short, the worldly.

And when I compare that with the wonder of reality as I have found it in the Lord Jesus Christ, well, it is like comparing a dark and stormy night following a great discouragement, with the brightness of a new and clear dawn with its promise of hope.

FAA Academy
Oklahoma City
Class 76-9
November 25, 1976

For Wendy:

SHE CALLED ME "DAD"

It frightened me, a little, when
she called me Dad, but then
what is a Dad, but one of those
who holds the healthy fear of God
and knows
he must be poignantly aware
of those whose hearts are placed
within his trust.

And so I must, and do,
while standing 'neath the watchful
eye of God,
accept the mantle, and am glad
that such a precious one
has called me "Dad."

Winchester, Oregon
September 10, 1985

THE ULTIMATE EXHILARATION

Three Christian brothers were sharing one day. "Fellas," Dean was saying, "There is just no exhilaration like sailing. Why, there you are, slicing up a cove, beside a gravel bar, in that magnificent Kachemak Bay in Alaska, seals watching, unafraid as you pass by. Ten times the wonder of the Alpine crags tower to the south; the ocean curves away to the north. Your sloop is heeling that perfect 15 degrees, and your towering sails are trimmed to perfection, lying in a curve that stirs the deepest part of a man, far deeper than those other curves you young fellows were speaking of.

"There is not a sound, save the rush of water by the hull, and the brush of the breeze through the rigging. Your small ship responds instantly, with a marvelous, intimate sensativity to the lightest touch of your hand on the helm. You are Captain in command in your own world.

"That is exhilaration."

Mark and Dave were listening with much more than polite attention. They were almost literally sailing, there, with their respected older brother.

With the spirit of true conversation upon them, they rested for several moments in that sharing.

Finally, though, Mark spoke. "I know what you are saying, Brother, but for me, it is flying. I tell you, man, when you are setting there on the end of a hot, long runway, your engine ticking over in that syncopated, idling sound that only an airplane engine has; and then it is your turn to go. That is living. You pour on the power, your ship accelerates down the black ribbon, rolling like any other earthbound machine, until flying speed is reached. And then you haul gently back on the wheel, and what was just moments before no more than a car or truck, is now a winged thing, lifting you up, up, into that wild and yonder, everlasting sky.

"You climb to 10 or 12 thousand feet, past the local cumulus clouds; you can see the curving earth, falling away for a hundred miles in any direction. The world is yours. I couldn't say it better than Lt. John Magee in his poem, "High Flight:" 'Up, up, up the long, delirious, burning blue, I've topped the wind-swept heights with easy grace, where never lark, nor even eagle, flew. And while, with silent, lifting mind I've trod the high, untrespassed sanctity of space, put out my hand, and touched the face of God.'

"Man, I tell you, that is exhilaration."

Again, the spirit of true conversation held them; three souls as one, there, in the endless sky.

Dave had been attentively listening with more than politeness. He had been caught up in his older brothers' enthusiasm. As the spell faded, it was David's turn. There was no doubt that God had given this fine, young man the body of a superb athlete. Lean and strong, he had practiced long and hard, eating well, leaving drugs, tobacco, and alcohol to the fools. In another year or two, he would be a candidate for the U.S. Olympic ski team.

He spoke, "I hear you, fellas, loud and clear; and I must say, 'Almost thou persuadest me to be a flyer, or a sailor.' But God gave me the magnificent gift of a healthy, athletic body. All I have to do is think a thought, and this body does marvelous things.

"Why, there you are; you've taken the lift to the top of the mountain. It is early morning; you are the first to go. It has been snowing all night, so that there are 12 to 14 inches of powder on top of 8 feet of partly packed snow. You are at 3000 feet, with nearly 8 miles of virgin snow ahead. You shove off, and fall, like a diving eagle, the wind you yourself are making, whistling by your helmet at from 30 to 60 miles per hour.

"A mile down comes the jump, a sharp drop in the trail, and for a hundred feet you are airborne, knowing exactly how you will land in an explosion of powder snow. And then the double S turns. Almost without thinking, your legs are springing to the uneven trail, your ankles turn, lightly, then steeply into the turns. Snow flies away for fifty feet to the left, and then to the right, and again left, and then right, but you stay in the center of that trail, and, almost like an observer, marvel at this 'fearfully and wonderfully made' machine, the human body.

"No disrespect, my brothers, but how can there be any exhilaration to top that?"

The three basked together, in the shared glory for awhile. Then the older man spoke, "You know, Brothers, we have each spoken, with very real enthusiasm about three, quite different activities. And yet, I think we have been talking about the same thing. It really is not the sailing, or flying, or skiing we long for; it is the exhilaration. And that is the same for each of us. David, maybe there is an exhilaration 'to top that,' although your recognition of the wonder of the human body, God's creation in motion, just about topped all three of us.

"But all through the Bible, Jesus is, in essence, saying this 'Know me, know my Father, and know a glorious exhilaration beyond *anything* this world can offer.'

"Didn't He, Himself, tell us this when He said, 'I came that you might have *life*, and have it more abundantly'? And He didn't mean just sailing, or flying, or skiing. He meant *life*.

"And didn't St. Paul say, 'For me to live, is Christ.'? With the long miles he walked, he must have been a superb athlete. He might even have crowded you, David, on the slopes. He had a fine mind, so certainly he could have learned flying; and been a good one. And the tents he made; surely he could have made sails, and used them well.

"And in his letter to the Philippians he made this astounding statement, '...I count all things but loss for the excellency of the knowledge of Christ Jesus, my Lord... and do count...all things but refuse...that I may know Him...'

"And then we are told in God's Word that He 'inhabits the praises of His people.' *God*, Almighty God inhabits those praises. Could there be any greater, any more glorious exhilaration than living with God?

"No, I am not saying that we should stop sailing, or flying, or skiing. I'm just saying, know what you are really seeking, and then of course, as God's Word says, 'covet earnestly the best...'"

Bastendorff Beach, Oregon
January 20, 1988

BEGINNING

How many countless words have been written about the early morning, the early morn, the dawn of a new day? How many will yet be written, or spoken, or sung, about this lovely hour? And I, I have the audacity to write still more?

Yes, yes, for the morning is birth, the morning is beginning, the morning is mine. Most of the real experiences of my life have been lived in the early morning hours: the glorious colors of sunrises in the Columbia Gorge where dark green mountains frame the morning sky; the peace and healing stillness of the cool, desert morning of eastern Oregon, or the same thundering silence wrapped around my cabin, here, on the shore of an Alaskan pond.

Birth is hope, birth is promise, and I thank God each morning for the birth of a new day. We see and feel this hope and promise with the birth of a child. With our past experiences and lessons learned, tied to the eager vitality of the new born, we have more than the right, we have the deadly real responsibility to hope for a better world, and this all holds just as true for the birth of a new day. I have lived before, but I have not lived this new and unknown, untried, unused new day. Birth is hope and promise.

And what is beginning but the greatest of all moments: the beginning of an ocean voyage with all the "far away places" to be seen and known; the beginning of college with all the strange and exciting fields of learning there to be walked upon; the beginning of a new job with its exciting challenges to our past training and experience; the beginning of a new love .

The morning is beginning,—and the morning is mine.

Lloyd's Pond, Alaska
Summer, 1968

FORWARD TO "WENDY'S STORY"

When I married Ramona, of course I married her entire family. And that included her precious, precious daughter, Wendy.

Wendy truly was a rare one; a so special one; surely, one of the "too few." Oh, she was physically beautiful, in fact, remarkably beautiful. But in every other way, she was a very ordinary young woman, with all of the "earthen vessel" flaws of any other.

But surely, our God had placed something most unique within her. For to know her, very literally was to love her. Or, more correctly, to know her was to discover that one was somehow privileged to love her. I think that Wendy was not at all aware of that fact. She was just Wendy.

But that subtle, yet penetrating glow flowed out from her, in an imperceptible, yet very real stream, so that often, even people who just heard about her as she was dying from Melanoma cancer, even they were drawn to ask with very real concern, "And how is Wendy?" Not, "How is your daughter?" but, "How is Wendy?"

So let the following story and ballad tell you about one of God's special sacrifices.

Dean Nichols

WENDY'S STORY

A few months ago, Wendy, knowing in her heart that she was going home, asked me to write a story about her and Michael. She gave me a few particulars and notes of some of the things that, she truly felt, made her years with this fine young man, a rich, "good life," filled with the material blessings of this world. But she wanted told, also, the richer blessings known of fidelity, of the absolute assurance from day one, that they two were meant for each other, of growth of character, and of an ever closer walk with our Lord.

She also asked that I write a poem for her; both the poem and the story to be read at this service today.

I think I just stalled for a while. But I just couldn't seem to pull anything together. But about two weeks ago, the seeds she had planted insisted on germinating, and I had no choice but to sit down, take up pen and paper, and let the words flow upon the page.

But the words, "poem," and "story," blended together. And what came forth was the following ballad; a ballad being a long poem that tells a story; or, perhaps, a story written in poetic form.

But I think that is good, because we get the story told, but we utilize the condensed power of poetry, with its imaging, its similes, its metaphors, all that compress deep concepts into very few words. So I ask you to listen carefully, missing not a word, or phrase; because, what Wendy and Michael have done for us all, in bearing this storm, is too precious to be lost. We must, we must let its arrow drive deeply into our own souls.

Months before she left us, but well after the cancer had put its mark upon her, Wendy knew, she knew, in the deep intimacy of that knowing, that the life, the price of her life that she was giving was insignificant, so very, very little, compared to the fullness, the quiet, filling glory of truly receiving, truly knowing the immeasurable richness of God's Peace.

Although, as she said, she could not describe that Peace, still its penetrating glow flowed out from her, not only to all who were close to her, but also to those, miles away, who just asked about her. She, and we, have paid a terrible price, in man's measure.

But Wendy would have us remember, that, if we will receive it, we can know, through her life, and death, much of that matchless treasure of peace, her life, the giving of her life, bought for her, and for us.

Dean Nichols
Autumn 1992

For Wendy Marie Moore
December 7, 1960—November 10, 1992

Photo by Terry Day, Roseburg, Oregon

A PEARL OF GREAT PRICE
(A ballad of victory)

"Why am I so blessed?" she asked one day.
And I could answer only, "'Tis God's plan."
Prophetic? I think not. The Word of God
abundantly declares that He
directs the course of man.

But then I heard these words come forth:
"It's for His purposes we live, you know.
And one day we shall know, and understand,
that when He asks a price of us,
that very asking is a gift, a gift,
and *not* a cruel demand."

The conversation, like a mist, was gone.
And years rushed on, as surely years can do.
We watched with joy, the blessings
that God poured upon her life:
a gracious personality that grew,
a beauty that matured,
               as roses do,
a husband, engineer by trade,
a handsome lad,
with dark, Italian countenance,
engaging smile,
but talent too, for which employers
gladly paid.

And she? The call was always there,
"Come, bring your grace, your dedication,
loyalty, and fine mind. This office needs
you, needs you, and your special kind."

But deeper than the blessings of this world,
she saw a bonding with her man,
that tied them to the Infinite;
and as our Lord unfurled
to her, His flag of Truth, she saw
yet deeper still, she and her man
were special to His will.

Oh yes, like any tree that grows,
their marriage knew the buffeting,
by winds that blew, and rains, and snows,
and scorching summer sun,
but yet it grew.
Its roots were deep, secure,
she knew, she knew.

But why? Again, her questing heart inquired:
That love, fidelity, and "paid for" things,
are qualities to be admired?
"Oh yes, that too," the Holy Spirit said,
as one dark night upon her bed,
she prayed that she be led.
"But one day soon," she heard Him say,
"I shall require of you, a sacrifice I ask
of but a very special few."

The years passed by, and then,
one day, along the ocean's sandy shore
she'd grown to love, where peace
so often came, and more;
we walked beside her and that endless sea
that speaks so well of His infinity.

The wind was blowing in her golden hair;
her lovely eyes held mystery, yet care,
and love, and deep compassion too
for those she knew.

We waited, there, upon the sand.
The poignant drama would demand
we listen both with heart and soul;
and then she spoke, "That tiny mole

the Surgeon's knife removed,
was Melanoma cancer, 'And,' they say, 'we
were too slow.
The cells have travelled far,
and all the science known to man
can never tell us where they are.'"

We all stood still, and listened
for His perfect will,
as deep inside
we felt the storm of fear,
and flood of peace,
collide.

But, one by one we heard the gentle call,
"Peace, peace, be still. *I* brought you here,
along the ocean's sandy shore
she's grown to love;
where peace is Mine to give, and more.
I brought you here;
so listen to My voice, and know,
you have a choice,
to fear,
or heed my sage advice, and know—
I choose the best, and only choose the best
for sacrifice."

We did not understand, but still,
we put our trust in Him,
and let the years again roll on.
We let the drama, there beside the sea,
become, almost, a distant memory.

And then, just one short year ago,
like lightning from the East,
the silent killer came.
"We find no other cancer in your frame,"
the Surgeon said.
"This one large tumor in your brain
we can remove.
And if we get it all, you could live on,
for years, until you hear your Master's call."

And so she gave him her consent
to operate, yet knew it meant
but brief reprieve.
For she *had* heard His call,
those many years ago,
which spoke into her heart,
"If you believe, I'll take you through
a storm of fire few receive.
But as you go, I'll give you peace
that fewer still can know.
And through your sacrifice, and faith,
I'll give a lost and dying world,
a vision of the depth of My great Love,
no other way can show."

"Why me?" she asked again.
And yet again that golden voice intoned,
"Because, it's only you I trust,
to bear this storm,
and tell the scoffer,
      and the just,
what you have learned."

So then, to every listening ear, she told
her story from a heart so strong and free:
"A vision of all life is mine;
I can so clearly see;
the price I pay is life itself,
but, long before it's done,
I see the balance of the scales,
and know that I have won.
The priceless pearl of peace *is* mine;
and all it cost was me."

                                            Dean Nichols
                                            October 1992

HEALING REST

A few weeks after we put our precious Wendy to rest, my cousin, Capt. Mark Nichols, offered us the use of his cabin for a few days. It is located in the village of Long Beach, Washington, only, as the following expression says, a dune away from the great Pacific Ocean.

A few others, special ones, of course, are invited, now and then to use it also. So we left a "Guest Book" there, with the invitation for each to make some entry of their visit. With our Wendy still deeply on our hearts, we made the first entry:

"There is healing in these simple, wooden walls. And, like the wet and driving rain against the window glass that washes all away our pain of loss, so too, the spirits of the ones before, who linger near, whisper peace into our weary souls, and we find rest.

"And just a dune away, the ceaseless, sounding sea calls to our troubled hearts, 'Like He Who made me, and Who drives the wind along, I know not what fatigue can be. The tumult and the storm are but my song.

"'So give to me your haunted, hurting hearts.

"'As those before have drawn from this abode, receive the rest that's now your greatest need; and let my strong arms carry all your load.'"

Long Beach, Washington
December 1, 1992

Section III
CHALLENGES

[Umpqua Valley Christian Fellowship: I love every woman in this Church very much. I stand in awe before the obvious nobility of women. With all the earnestness I possess, I urge you to remember that, as you listen to, or read this prophesy. I like men, real men; and I like being a man. But I often stand in awe before that special, innate nobility in women.]

HATH GOD [REALLY] SAID?

"Wives, submit yourselves unto your own husbands, as unto the Lord." Ephesians 5:22. "...and let the wife see that she reverence her husband." Verse 33.

The Eves of today are still quoting the Serpent. And the Adams of today are still eating the apple.

The insidious infection of Feminism is still running rampant in the social fabric and in the Church.

A couple of weeks back, I read aloud from the Pulpit Ephesians 5:22-33, from the King James Bible. Then I read the same verses from the Living Bible. Then I read the same verses from the Amplified Bible.

There *are* Scriptures that come to us with a certain ambiguity, due to the difficulty of translating perfectly the intent of the writer of 2000 years ago. But the above Scriptures leave no such ambiguity. In fact, all three versions support each other fully, with one, small exception: The Living Bible paragraphs verse 21 with the remaining 12. This is obviously incorrect. Verse 21 is referring to the broad, general instruction for Christians to defer, wherever possible, to one another. Verses 22-33, are referring to that "Husband-Wife relationship" between "...Christ and the Church," Verse 32.

After the meeting, not one person, male or female, commented to me on that reading. It seemed to me at the reading, that many were intently listening, but not one person commented to me afterward.

But a day or two later, I was purchasing some items from a store owned by a lovely, female Saint of our Church. She had not been at the meeting when I read. In good humor, I told her what I had read.

She laughed, but there was no mistaking the Feminist rebellion when she threw up her hands, and declared, "Oh no, we're *not* going back to that."

"Hath God [really] said?"

Other Christian sisters have declared with the same fervor, "We are equal; we are equal."

True, when we get to heaven, there will be neither male nor female—when we get to Heaven. But here, clearly, we go by God's order.

The word, "submit," as used in Verse 22, is a military term, showing the similarity in order in the family to the order that the military *must* have in the service. The Sergeant *must* submit to the Lieutenant. The Sergeant may be younger, or older, better looking, stronger, more intelligent, better educated, even with a better singing voice; but for him to fail to submit to the military order would be anarchy and chaos. Is it any wonder that there is anarchy and chaos in our marriages today?

Far too often we hear the women of the Church declare, "Husbands, back off; we are equal. Our Church doctrine says so." But the screaming declaration, "We are equal!" flies in the face of the unmistakable command of God in verse 23, "For the husband is head of the wife, *even as* Christ is the head of the Church...," [Emphasis added], and verse 32, "...But I speak concerning Christ and the Church." Is the Church "equal" with Christ? I think not. And if not, then wives are *not* equal with husbands in the family order.

"Hath God [really] said?"

And what about women teaching men?

1 Tim. 2:12 (King James Bible): "But I permit not a woman to teach... the man..."

1 Tim. 2:12 (Living Bible): "I never let women teach men... Let them be silent in your Church meetings.

1 Tim. 2:12 (Amplified Bible): "I allow no woman to teach or have authority over men; she is to remain in quietness, and keep silence [in religious assemblies.]"

Ah, but, "Hath God [really] said?"

Oh I know that there are wives, a few, far too few, but a few who reverence their husbands, as Ephesians 5:33 commands, but, sadly, I know not one. Still, even King Lemuel made the plaintive cry, "Who can find a virtuous woman? For her price is far above rubies."

Until the men and women of the Church in general, and husbands and wives in particular, learn to operate their relationships as ordained by God, the Church will *never* become that "glorious Church, not having spot or wrinkle..." The "Bride" will *never* be "ready for the Groom."

Whom are we going to believe, Almighty God, Who wrote the Book; or the Serpent, who asked the taunting question, "Hath God [really] said?"

Bastendorff Beach, Oregon
June 16, 1989

ADULTERY IN HIS HEART

"The laws of Moses said, 'You shall not commit adultery.' But *I* say, 'Anyone who even looks at a woman with lust in his eye has already committed adultery with her in his heart.'" The words of Jesus, Matt. 5:27–28 (Living Bible)

[That the above equally applies to women, needs no amplification here.]

But have we, licentious beings that we be, allowed God to draw the fine line, to focus in our minds the laser beam of His light, to hone our awareness of His perfection to the razor edge that that above Scripture is meaning to do?

I think not.

In Psalm 79, verse 5 (Amplified Bible), we read, "How long, O Lord? Will you be angry forever? Shall your jealousy, which cannot endure a divided allegiance, burn like fire?"

Surely, surely He is telling us, "Even the slightest hint of sensual expression outside of marriage is 'divided allegiance.'" And has He not, over, and over, likened earthly marriage, with its commanded fidelity, to our commitment to Him?

Sensuality of any kind is of the flesh. In Matt. 19:5 we are told, "...And the two shall be one flesh."

Therefore, *any* expression of sensuality outside of this very special, very narrow, most unique union, is a violation of this commandment, for commandment it is.

Matthew 5, from verse 21 on is saying again, and again, "You have heard that it was said by them of old... But *I* say unto you..." And the last verse, "Be you, therefore, perfect, as your Father Who is in Heaven is perfect." And again from His Word, "...narrow is the gate, and hard is the way which leads unto life..." Jesus came to fine tune us.

It has increasingly become clear to this grey haired observer, that God is drawing His people into an even closer, ever narrower walk with Him, an even *finer* tuning of His people. Some, who hold this narrow view, have been called prudes. But if we are, then we must agree that God Himself is a prude. He is the One who said, "...narrow is the gate."

The Puritans, in their standoff, very proper manners with one another, understood this, and so handed down to us a remarkable, moral strength. And we should be grateful to them.

But now, today, in this ever narrowing walk into which He is leading us, He is, at the same time, through our hugging in our Churches, through our expressions of warm affection between Christian Brothers and Sisters, He is walking us closer to a line, a nebulous, so difficult to define line. But it is a line that says, "On this side, your contact with another, whether with body, hand, mouth, or even eye, is filial, or at most, warmly affectionate; but over that line, the contact is sensual, and therefore abhorrent to a God Who created sex, who created sensuality, but Who so honored this creation that He licensed it between man and wife alone.

Oh, I know, a kiss on the mouth *can* be only "warmly affectionate." And in the culture of some families, and between family members, it is that only. But in this day of increasing communicable diseases, the most insidious of which is AIDS, I truly believe, God is warning us. Any kiss on the mouth will exchange *some* body fluids. However loudly the apologists for Homosexuality may shout to the contrary, AIDS, and of course, many other diseases, *can* be communicated by a kiss on the mouth.

But even this is not the primary, the fundamental reason for reserving kissing on the mouth for one's spouse exclusively.

The fundamental, primary, bottom line reason is: God said (in paraphrase,) "You shall have sensual contact with no one but the one I have licensed you to contact sensually." And this very clearly includes hugging another, or even looking or smiling in any other than a filial, or at the most, in a warmly affectionate way. And God will know which it is.

Kissing, hugging, or looking that has the slightest sensuality to it, has to be "lusting" in this fine tuned sense.

How do we totally avoid sinning in this "Adultery In His Heart" area? We can't, perfectly; and God knows that. He created us as sensual beings. But He did say, in effect, "Don't dwell there; don't play at it." Or, as He told Timothy, "Flee youthful lusts; when they pop into your consciousness, flee them."

I remember one time in a restaurant in Anchorage, Alaska, coming face to face with a young

Feminist. She had a sign on her chest which read, "What are you looking here for, Jack?" She had that written on a tight fitting sweatshirt, well displaying a remarkably well developed pair of mammary glands. As a male animal, I saw them. But I said, "I am reading your sign. There is nothing else worthy of my attention." Ok, so it was a caustic comeback, and as a Christian, I apologize. But the look of consternation on her face was almost startling. The Feminist in her had been made the fool; but the woman in her had been hurt.

I remember another time, in our Church, just before the Service began, hugging a lovely young woman in her forties, about the age of my youngest daughter. We loved each other as close friends, and do to this day. But that evening, for the briefest of moments, that hug felt good in a way not allowed by our Lord. We had crowded that line, and we knew it. We have never spoken of it, nor need we, but for a few weeks after that, we didn't hug each other at all. We had properly fled.

Just the other day, in Church, as the choir walked on stage to sing, I remarked to my wife, "Look at that figure on that beautiful young woman." And she agreed. There was nothing lustful, nor sensual about the observation. No, clearly, our Lord is not telling us to be blind; but we are to flee, flee, flee any hint of sensuality outside of the marriage bond; we are to reject immediately any temptation to express the slightest sensual contact with one other than husband or wife. For to do so is to commit adultery in our hearts.

Fidelity, faithfulness, trustworthiness, must be among the highest of desires of God for His people. Look up Trustworthiness, fidelity, faithfulness in your Strong's Concordance, and in your Thompson Chain Reference, and see why the tears of God will flow, when He, Who is faithful, sees us faithlessly commit adultery, even in our hearts.

Bastendorff Beach, Oregon
April 4, 1989

GOD'S ORDER

"Let all things be done decently and in order."
1 Cor. 14:40

Exceptions

A woman can do anything in the Church that a man can do, if, I repeat, *if* she has a bona fide Holy Spirit directed instruction from God to make, or be, an *exception* to God's General Rule.

It must always be remembered that an exception would not be an exception if it were not an exception; and, an exception does *not* make a new General Rule.

Questions

1. Is the Bible true?
2. If we answer yes, then we must ask: When it is crystal clear what the Bible is telling us, are we to do the best we can to act according to that commandment, or, if we don't like that particular Scripture, may we just sweep it under the rug?
3. If we say yes to the first part of question 2 above, then we must ask: Is it clear that women are

not to teach men, as a general rule, or, act in any way in authority over men?

4. As we all know, there are exceptions all through the Bible, but, is the exception we may be considering; such as, a woman preaching, or teaching a Sunday School Class, is the one we are considering a bona fide exception, called by the Holy Spirit?

5. And can we accept as a given that the *only* One Who can make an exception to God's Commandments, God's General Rules, is God Himself through the Holy Spirit?

6. Dare we, licentious beings though we be, dare we ever defy our God by turning one of His "exceptions" into a new General Rule?

Never, never, never.

April, 1991

GOD'S PERFECT ORDER

Men, and women, are identical.

In God's economy, we each add up to 100 percent. And 100 percent, and 100 percent, are two, identical numbers.

"Of course," I hear you say, "Any dummy can see that."

But, let me explain:

When we get to Heaven, there are neither male nor female. Matt. 22:30. We will see each other as either, 100% or 100%. *When* we get to Heaven.

But God, Who is all seeing, sees us, even now, as 100% and 100%.

But when He created man, He created man (the flesh) male *and* female. Gen. 1:27.

Psychologists, secular, *and* Christian have fully agreed that, clearly, by definition there are, in the natural, the flesh, "masculine" characteristics and "feminine" characteristics. Example: Whipping out a sword and fighting to the death is a masculine characteristic. Giving clear, decisive commands and expecting them to be carried out is a masculine characteristic. (There are a number of others, of course.) But when a woman finds herself in a situation where either of the above characteristics is needed, such as, defending her children or ordering their day's work, or such, she is, by necessity, utilizing a couple of the masculine characteristics that God, Himself, placed within her. But these are "masculine" characteristics.

Another example: Nursing a sick or injured or hurting one, child, adult, or aged one, is a "feminine" characteristic. (And again, by agreed-on definition among both secular *and* Christian Psychologists.) Sensitively, emotionally, responding to beauty (sunsets, flowers, an awesome view of the Grand Canyon or the Oregon Coast), or being stirred by the lovely strains of music that reaches into the soul, this sensitive responding is a feminine characteristic. What man, what very real, virile male animal would call himself a man, and never exhibit, at an appropriate time, of course, such lovely, feminine characteristics? But they *are* "feminine" characteristics.

But God's Word abundantly, abundantly declares, that, although in *His* economy, 100% equals 100%, in *this* life male and female are *not* the same.

I think that we can readily agree that, in God's structure, the following formula would be much more intricate and involved; but just for the purposes of this prophesy, let us simplify the formula:

Male: 95% plus 5% equals 100%.

Female: 5% plus 95% equals 100%.

The first numbers are "masculine" characteristics. The second numbers are "feminine" characteristics. Male and female each add up to 100%, but the ratios are, and should be, reversed. It is not, obviously, the occasional utilization of characteristics of the opposite sex that disturbs, or perverts God's Order. It is the carrying of that ratio beyond God's plan, or, as the Feminists, Satan's amazingly effective angels, have tried to do, removing that ratio entirely.

The "Uni-sex" movement promoted for awhile with some success and raw audacity by Feminists, Homosexuals, and Lesbians, had as its aim the total elimination of God's order, *His* ratio.

And all over the world, statistics are showing that women, who have moved up into positions of high authority in the Church as well as in the world, are bailing out of those positions by the thousands. No, the news media, which itself is perverted, is not telling this. On the contrary, they point again and again to the relatively few who stay in those positions and/or are doing a fine job there.

But deeper study will show that, in most cases, these last are exceptions to God's General Rule. And it is written: An *exception*, even one approved of by God, is an *exception*. And an *exception* does *not* establish a new General Rule.

But what of those bailing out? The studies further show that, in order to carry out the responsibilities of command, masculine characteristics must be exercised. And when one sex is so placed in circumstances that demand the exercising of too many characteristics of the opposite sex, or the use of those characteristics is demanded to a degree beyond God's plan for that one, then that one, the wise ones at least, recognize that they become, in a true sense, perverted. The women studied did not want to lose their God-given femininity. And they were wise enough to know that, if they stayed, that perversion of God's perfect order would occur.

Of course, women are equal to men in God's view. One hundred percent certainly equals 100 percent.

But in the social fabric that *He* designed, in the family order that *He* designed, equal does *not* mean same. And God's Word abundantly, abundantly declares that, just as in the Military where God views the Sergeant as 100%, and the Captain as 100%, for purposes of order, the Sergeant is secondary to the Captain. And so it is in the social fabric, and in the family, the woman is secondary to the man. 1 Peter 3:1 and 3:5 (Amplified Bible). In the flesh, woman was made for man, not man for woman. 1 Corinthians 11:9, any version.

It is *not* being chauvinistic to insist on all of this. Is it chauvinistic to insist, even fight for the concept that God's Order, *God's* Order, be complied with? As the Holy Spirit has insisted in previous prophesies through my hand, God's Word repeatedly likens the relationship between Christ and the Church, to the relationship between Husband and Wife. Ephesians 5:32.

And until mankind gets *that* (Husband-Wife, male-female) relationship right, he simply *cannot* be that "Glorious Church without spot or wrinkle." His relationship with God will *not* be that perfect one that He designed. It is that perfect *relationship* that this writer yearns for with every fibre of his being, not, not, not, simply male dominance over women.

God's lovely, and perfect order must be *our* goal.

October 3, 1991

A HARSH OPINION

[Although the story that follows may seem harsh, it is not my intent in the slightest to injure or offend anyone. You may differ with me, but these are my honest observations. I believe in noble dreams; I cry when they are lost.]

The Democratic Party, Labor Unions, Abortion Rights Groups, The American Civil Liberties Union, The League Of Women Voters, The National Organization For Women, our Public Schools System: Seven institutions with one thing in common—no, two. They began with, ostensibly, noble motives; and two, I was, at one time or another (though no longer), either a member of, or a strong supporter of each one.

But all seven have one more thing in common. To greater or lesser degree, they each have degenerated into destructive institutions.

Oh, one would not wish to argue with the assertion that "There are well-meaning people, even now, within those organizations." With the exception of N.O.W., I would not argue with that assertion.

The Democratic Party, saying, as it should, that it was concerned about "people" still allowed its leaders to stifle initiative, cripple free enterprise, and make dirty words of very proper terms such as profit and corporation. This degeneration is a sad loss.

The Union Movement, building at first on the principles of safe working conditions, reasonable hours, and quality work for quality pay, degenerated, generally, into selfish, self-centered organizations, making virtue of "demanding rights," and building a camaraderie out of an us-against-them attitude, which, in turn, destroyed, or at least badly damaged their capacity for such true virtues as loyalty, productivity, and quality workmanship. In most cases, a noble dream is lost.

That the Abortion Rights Groups had noble motives in the beginning may be harder to say; but looking at my own involvement, one would have to say that, for those, like myself at one time, who have not thought it through, it would indeed appear reasonable that a "woman has a right to her own body." But when they say that, they ignore one of God's most crucial commands, "Thou shalt not spill innocent blood." Our murder of over fifteen million innocent babies is worse than the Nazi Holocaust, and second only to the ongoing murders of over 60 million of their own people by the Communists. This perversion of human rights, like any perversion, is a loss; of innocence only, perhaps, but still a loss.

The A.C.L.U., beginning as a champion of the little guy against bureaucratic oppression, has degenerated into a machine for advancing the self-centered, and self-destructive, tenets of "me-ism," implying, or even asserting that "the Government" is automatically evil, and especially the concept of a capitalistic, representative Republic, is, according to their spokesmen, inherently wrong. The A.C.L.U. seems to treat rebellion as the only true virtue. A champion is gone. Did we here lose a true champion?

The League of Women Voters, drawing on the noble, inherent virtues of womanhood, such as a desire for peace, order, stability, honesty, and a natural, greater concern for others than self, built a respected, credible organization. But they did not build, within their beginnings, a defense against the clever, subvertive, designs of the Feminist/Humanist forces that slipped in, and degenerated them into just another arm of Feminism, attempting, surreptitiously of course, to split God's design of perfect harmony between man and woman, into two warring camps. Sadly, the League of Women Voters can no longer be taken seriously by any thinking man or woman. What a loss.

Knowing the true beginning of the National Organization For Women, it would be wrong to state that it had noble motives. Betty Friedan, the founder, is one of the signers of the Humanist Manifesto II, the "Bible" of the Humanist movement. She knew very well what she was doing, waging a deliberately, destructive war on the Bible and the family, God's fundamental building block of *His* social fabric.

But for several years the organization flourished on the apparently noble motives of righting a few wrongs, (most of which were in the process of being righted anyway), and righting many perceived "wrongs" that were not wrongs at all; such as, a woman staying home and building and nurturing the nest and family, while her husband went out into the "exciting" world of sweat and stress and worry, beating the business bushes for enough money to feed, clothe, and house his family. The N.O.W. did not really degenerate. It just was in a relatively short time exposed for what it really is. And truly wise women have left its ranks by over 80 percent of its one time membership. Yes, the N.O.W. has been instrumental in "raising the consciousness of American women," but not at all in the destructive way they intended. What Satan meant for evil, God has meant for good, and American women are now joining, by the hundreds of thousands, such truly noble organizations as Concerned Women for America, and other groups that give support to women who want to be women as God designed them to be. This has been no loss.

But by far the most influential of the seven, the Public Schools System began, like N.O.W., with ignoble motives. Horace Mann, often called the Father of Public Education, is often quoted as saying, in effect, "We shall make of the Public Schools for Humanism what the Church has been for Christianity." And supporting that concept, Gloria Steinham, prominent Feminist and Editor of *Ms. Magazine*, said in a speech in Houston, Texas, "This will be the first revolution in history financed by the enemy." And for Gloria Steinham, Christianity and the traditional family are the enemy.

But unlike N.O.W., which, in overall history, will appear as no more than an irritating flash in the pan, the Public Schools System was built, slowly, carefully, even slyly, using, as with the League of Women Voters, the well-established bases of family, moral values, patriotism, free enterprise, the work ethic, and such. The hundreds of thousands of Educators recruited into the system brought with them noble motives. But again like the League, they were innocently, if ignorantly, unaware of the long range goals of Horace Mann, and such Humanists as John Dewey, another signer of the Humanist Manifesto, and a more modern "Father" of Public Education.

It has been well said, "The only thing necessary for evil to triumph is for good men to do nothing." And so our truly noble educators have been, over the years, used to give a noble appearance to "Education," while the Humanists, again working surreptitiously behind the scenes, have almost totally driven Christianity (the enemy) out of our schools and replaced it with the atheistic values of Humanism. Their own documents declare this as their intent. And then, sometimes they even brag that their moves are so bizzare, they can declare them openly and no one will believe them. For example, here in Roseburg, Oregon a little over a year ago, at a dinner at the Moose Lodge for the Citizen of the Year Award, Homer Duncan, head of the Oregon Department of Education, had the arrogant audacity to say in his speech, "We [really] are not Educators, we are Change Agents." That is the term used in training teachers (as many teachers, that is, as can be trusted with this "secret") to get them to "realize" that it is their *primary* duty to change the values of our children from the "decadent values of their parents," to the "progressive" values of the "New Age."

And textbooks are being radically changed to reflect Humanist/Socialist, even Communist values, while *any* contribution of Christianity to the history of this nation is being deliberately removed.

As the drama of this very real, truly sinister conspiracy to capture the minds of our children is being played out, the sleeping giant of real America is wakening. Parents, in their wise efforts to take their children out of such a system of "Values Clarification" (as the Humanists call it) are establishing private, mostly Christian Schools at the rate of three a day. That's 21 a week, 84 a month, over 1000 a year.

And the quality of education they are trading for? A study, commissioned by no less than the Oregon Department of Education, to study private schools in Oregon, found, among many very interesting things, that in general, the private schools were providing better education, with higher SAT scores and at approximately one-third the cost of the Public Schools.

So what is the conclusion? Abolish the Public Schools System? No, I think we cannot do that without throwing the baby out with the dirty water. Like the other six organizations, no, five, I cannot include N.O.W., but like the other five, there are many, moral, patriotic, traditional family oriented people in "Education," who need our help in recapturing what once was a noble establishment. The Freedom Council, represented in most cities, and the National Legal Foundation, c/o The 700 Club, Virginia Beach, VA 23463, can give council; and the National Assn. of Christian Educators, P.O. Box 3200, Costa Mesa, CA 92626, can help.

We can push our legislators for the Voucher System, so that parents can choose the school they want for their children, whether Public or private. (We already have precedence in that we give grants to students to attend private colleges.) But the Vouchers must have no strings attached. The *only* criteria for deciding which schools may receive the vouchers must be the criteria set by the parents or guardians themselves. This system, like the entire free enterprise system, will force all schools, public and private, to deliver or go out of business.

It has been well said, "Influence has greater power than authority." Surely, the honorable profession of teaching has, by the hours involved, but also by its very nature, the filling of absorbent minds, a greater influence on the entire course of human events than any other profession. To be true to its terrible responsibility, the profession of teaching absolutely demands dedication, but dedication free to listen to the Holy Spirit of God, the greatest teacher of all time. And this freedom has been or is being stolen.

And so we can push our legislators to outlaw the teacher's union, the N.E.A. It is well documented that this organization is dominated by Humanists. No conscientious, truly dedicated educator can be free to stimulate, constructively, the minds of students while that teacher is hounded by a private organization whose values are counter to God, to traditional American Family values. To lose our schools is to lose America; we cannot lose our schools.

Seven institutions, there are many, many more. But these seven are evidence that we can be duped. And it smarts to have to admit that; I know, I've been there. But as it is written, "A wise man can change his mind; only a fool never does."

April, 1988

"And a vision appeared to Paul in the night; there stood a man... beseeching him, and saying, 'Come over into Macedonia, and help us.'"

Acts 16:9

ONE HUNDRED BOATS FOR THE PHILIPPINES

A Scattering Of Seed

This is *not* an appeal for money or donations. It *is* an appeal for your careful reading, and then your prayer, if no more than one breath, "Lord, what part do you want me to have in this, if anything?"

Of course, if the Holy Spirit asks you to pray more, then please pray for the development of this vision into reality.

And neither is it my intention, with this story, to even be planting seeds; but rather to just be scattering them, and leaving it to the Wind of Heaven to carry them to fertile ground. So for now, just enjoy reading a story.

The Vision

I had a vision. Well, not really a vision vision. It was more one of those kinds of ideas that come to you, but will not go away.

I was retired, age 65, but in good health. I had a modest retirement income; I had surrendered my whole being to the Lordship and service of Jesus about 12 years before; and, with over 42 years in the labor force of this great land, I had accumulated considerable skills and experience in handling boats of many kinds and sizes, both power and sail. For several years, I had pondered the question, "How can I put this all together in the service of our Lord?"

The Shipyard

Up on Whidbey Island in Washington State is a small shipyard operated by my first cousin, Frank's, two sons, Matt Nichols, President, and Archie Nichols, Vice President and Chief Design Engineer. Although they are cousins, because Frank and I are closer than brothers, the two "boys" generally call me "Uncle Dean."

A Seed Is Planted

A couple years ago, after the second or third visit at our Church, by Pastor Benito Pacleb, President of the Full Gospel Fellowship of Churches and Ministers of the Philippines, several pieces of knowledge fell together: There are over 7000 islands in the Philippines, with no roads between them; there are 58 million people spread over those islands, and, not only are those lovely, alert people hungry for the Gospel in its uncomplicated truth, free of idolatry, they are eager to take that message to the rest of the Orient. In fact, Filipino workers are hired for jobs all over the world. They have a freer access to the rest of the world, especially the Orient, than do Americans.

After the meeting, I asked Pastor Pacleb if I could have a few minutes of his time. He not only granted the time, but, in his unique way, he gave his total, undivided attention.

I gave him a brief summary of my retirement situation, my commitment to Jesus, my skills and knowledge, and a bit about my connections with this small shipyard.

"Pastor," I urged, "Please grasp this first word: If, I repeat, *if* I could get my cousins to build me a boat, could you use it, and me, in evangelistic work in the Philippines?" (I was thinking of perhaps a 30- or 40-foot, auxiliary-powered sailboat.)

Although his serious face gave almost no show of emotion, he did answer, "Let me think about it." I gave him my name and address.

Go Ye Yourself

A couple months went by. My zeal had cooled. Secretly I thought, "That was a kind of wild idea. I'm not really qualified for such a venture. Maybe he has forgotten the idea, because it is indeed impractical. Good, I'm off the hook; I'll find something closer to home."

But then came a letter from Pastor Pacleb, which said, in effect, "I have taken up your suggestion with my board. The consensus is that that would be the fulfillment of our own vision here. However, we would need a larger boat than you suggested; we would need one that could carry a small jeep, a big tent, and up to 150 people."

I looked up to Heaven and asked, "What now, Lord?" And then I shared the letter with my Pastor, Don Franke.

At his suggestion, we drove to Harrisburg for a conference with Leon Willis, President of the Full Gospel Fellowship of Churches and Ministers of Oregon. President Leon had some good questions, and some words of caution, but he could and would not suggest we abandon the dream, which was becoming a vision.

So Pastor Don and I drove to Whidbey Island where we had a serious meeting with Matt Nichols, the President of the Shipyard, and my first cousin, Frank. It was important to me to have Frank there. I respected his blunt but wise and telling counsel.

We presented the vision, and the developments so far.

Matt is not President of a buzzing shipyard by accident. He does not waste words.

"Uncle Dean," he asked, "Why me? This company lost over two million dollars last year, and we can't do that two years in a row. We couldn't build you a rowboat right now."

But I really wasn't asking him to build me a boat at this time. I was just doing the best I could at following the Holy Spirit's directions, and was presenting the vision, and the need.

So I said, "Matt, I know that Jesus is Lord in your life, so I am not asking *you* to make the decision. I am just asking that, if the Holy Spirit directs you to, will you build this boat?"

The firm lines on the face of this young Captain of industry softened as he quietly answered, "Uncle Dean, if the Holy Spirit tells me to build you a boat, we'll build you a boat."

Cousin Frank had been quietly listening during the hour long discussion. He spoke, "I can't argue with your vision, but how sure are you of the need? Could a boat be bought, or built there *much* more cheaply? I think you, yourself should go over there and check it out in person. I'd even be willing to help a bit on your trip."

We all concurred; Matt took Pastor Don and me on a tour of the yard, and then the two of us left on the 400-mile drive home. I had Frank's check in my pocket. Obviously, I was going to the Philippines.

I borrowed as much again, and in May of '86, Pastor Don and I, Brother Milt Atkisson, Pastor C. L. Henry, and Brother Alvin Lee were accompanying President Leon Willis: Destination, Dumaguete City and the Southern Philippines.

The Prophesy

A few weeks before we left, Evangelist Bob Curry was visiting and preaching one evening in our Church. Surely, this man *is* a man of God. Surely, if there is a Prophet in these times, Bob Curry is one.

After the preaching, and an alter call came, I felt clearly led of the Holy Spirit to go forward and ask Bob for prayer concerning the vision. He listened intently to my very brief summary. Then he closed his eyes, listening, listening; and then this huge man put one hand on my chest, and, leaning down with his face close to mine, spoke these words, "You are to press onward. Here and there, or now and then, God will close a door; but when He does, He will tell you why."

I stored this prophesy in my heart, and rode the silver wings, 6000 miles across the sea to the "City of Gentle People," and the home of Benito and June Pacleb. "I want you all to stay in our home," Benito said, "So we can fellowship."

But as we shared the first, week-long Seminar at the Bible School, the "Round House" with its five acres of land they are now renting; as we touched, hugged, worshipped with, prayed with, yes, and cried with these lovely, lovely brothers and sisters, we also learned the hard facts of the material world, and how they affect the work of the ministry.

Although they were succeeding, barely, but they were succeeding in raising the rent of nearly 400 U.S. dollars a month, they could not add the needed buildings, shops, dormitories, and classrooms, unless they owned the property.

The Bible School is really not a part of this story, so may I just brush over it with these few words. Somehow it tumbled into my lap, the task of attempting to raise the really fair price the owner was asking. "I really think," Benito said one evening as we were sharing in his quiet home, "that much as we need that boat, this school should come first." Yes, we all agreed.

An hour later, I was sitting alone at the table, and suddenly tears were flowing down my cheeks as, in my spirit, I heard again, the words of the Prophet of God, "You are to press onward. Here and there, or now and then, God will close a door; but when He does, He will tell you why." A door had been closed on my vision for awhile.

A Light Begins To Glow

I stayed with the team, of course, for the next two weeks, helping in a quiet way with the Crusades and Seminars around those isles of the sea. Occasionally,

I had the opportunity to study the local boats, the shipyards, the needs. Sometimes I gave my own testimony and something of the vision, although I surprised myself, or more correctly, the Holy Spirit surprised me as He prompted me to tell those people, "America cannot do it all. *If* we manage to get a boat over here, *you* will have to supply it with fuel, and food, and other supplies. And with all my heart, I believe you can." And as they grasped those words, I saw a light, small, but very real, begin to glow in the, eyes of some beautiful, Filipino people.

The Islands Call Again

We came home and a year flew by, as years have a way of doing. My efforts at raising money for the purchase of the Bible School, several as they were, each seemed even worse than running into a wall. It even seemed that they were flung back into my face. And so I drew back, licked my wounds, and waited. And as I said, a year flew by. The Philippines were calling again.

"Don," I told my Pastor, "I don't think I'll go this time. My boat project is dead in the water; I have nothing for the Bible School; I have books to finish and get published."

"I understand," he answered, "I really do. But every letter I receive, urging *me* to come, also asks, 'Is Brother Dean coming with you?'"

And so, with President Leon Willis and his precious wife, Latena, we flew again, across the vast

Pacific to that tiny, single, concrete ribbon called Dumaguete Airport, and into the arms and hearts of those lovely people.

Hard Work

It was much harder work this time. The "bug" bugged us, the heat oppressed us (Even the Filipinos complained of the heat), the shortage of water nagged at us and the local food was harder to endure. *And*, I never found the opportunity to further investigate my boat project, or even talk it over with that incredibly busy man, Benito Pacleb—until the last day. But more of that later.

In the meantime, we could not help but also see the great good our presence there was doing. The local congregations, and the weary Pastors were being encouraged; the fire of the Holy Spirit was being set free again; the fabric of the fellowship of believers across an ocean was being rewoven. And our own faith was being strengthened as miracles of healing came from the touch of our hands in Jesus' Name.

A brief excerpt from my Journal for May 15, in Surigao, will amplify this. "At the 9:00 A.M. session, Pastor Don preached on praise and worship. It set this Convention on fire. The Church will hold about 700 people, and was full morning and afternoon; but it was packed out this evening.

"Still, I was very mindful of what precious co-traveler, Pastor David Fuller had said, 'When God puts a call upon one's life, He is ruthless with the flesh.' Certainly my flesh longed to be home, where the smells are clean, the food fresh and to our taste, where the water, cold and hot, runs freely, where the language is readily understood, where we feel secure, and life around us is familiar, where toilet paper is ample, and does not fall apart in one's hands; the 'good life,' God's blessed American, good life. Certainly my flesh longed for home. And added to that, my own ministry here seemed vaguely defined, if not outright redundant. While the flow of praise, and worship around me, the anointing of the Holy Spirit upon the congregation poured out in an abundant flood, my body was poignantly aware that I was very weary, and, I had a stomach ache. What possible use can my spirit be to anyone in this context?

"Yet through it all, a subtle, yet undeniable message stayed close to my spiritual ear: 'Your very existence, your patient presence here puts body to the work of My swordsmen; and these Filipinos see you, attentive, patient, loving. But most of all, though you speak not a word, they hear, sense, feel My Love emanating from you. Deny yourself, and follow Me. Can the pot say to the Potter, 'Why have you made me thus?'"

A Day Off?

[Again from my Journal] "Surigao City, Mindanao, The Philippines, May 17, 1987: The Mission is over; we have tomorrow off, and then the long circle home, home to America, home to that blessed land.... In the restaurant this evening, we met an American couple, Dan and Susie Heinzman, with YWAM, (Youth With A Mission), and with them, a Filipino Dentist-Pastor Dr. Ben Asas. We fell in love as we shared my vision, and, YWAM's vision for these islands. Dan Heinzman said that he wanted me to meet a half American-Filipino who lives here, and is developing a small ministry called Inter-Island Christian Ministries. Tomorrow.

"Monday, May 18, 1987: A day off? Benito got us out about 6:30A.M. At breakfast, he and I finally had a short time to talk about 'the boat.' 'Oh yes, it is still greatly needed. No, we have not at all cooled on the dream.'

"Then he and most of the team headed for the airport, and home to Dumaguete.

Tidal turbulence among the islands.

"Dan Heinzman came in right then with Dr. Asas, and Albert Tracy, the half American-Filipino. We liked each other. They wanted to take me out to his, Tracy's, Barangay, San Jose, and show me the typical villages, channels, landings, along the way.

"So Dr. Asas met me at 11:00. We took a petticab to the port, and we caught a 'ferry,' about a 40-foot outrigger with cabin and motor, but no reverse. There were 25 to 30 people aboard. The toilet was a small 'outhouse' hanging over the stern.

"We ran the winding, often swiftly flowing, sometimes boiling channels, about 10 to 15 miles east to San Jose. There were stops along the way, of course. Sometimes the landing was a sort of dock, sometimes just the coral beach. We had walked a wobbly, 2 x 10 plank aboard in Surigao, and the same wobbly plank ashore onto the coral jetty at San Jose. Clearly

Debarking to San Jose.

One Hundred Boats For The Philippines

Bus service among the islands.

I saw the conditions under which our boat would work.

"We had some excellent sharing, mostly about the incredible need for a boat ministry in the islands. Our 60-foot Catamaran, carrying a couple Boston Whalers, still seemed like the best design. It must be steel, and with a tough bottom that could often rest on coral gravel or rocks over a tide. They told me that the last missionary boat had been to San Jose in 1974, 13 years ago.

"Missionary boats have almost unbelievable impact when they come," Albert told us, "But 13 years is too long." That last was clearly an understatement.

"As we looked at the marine charts that Albert had in his home, and saw the thousands of islands, with the untouched peoples on them, a shocking realization came crashing into my mind. 'Fellas,' I said, 'We don't need one boat for the Philippines; we need a hundred. When we draw a circle on these charts that would keep one boat fully occupied, we realize we could draw a hundred more.' With innocent simplicity, they all agreed, 'Yes, that is so.'

"I half laughed, half groaned, as I said, 'Good Grief, fellas, I have no idea where I'm going to get the half million dollars or so for one boat. Now we need a hundred. That's 50 million dollars.'

"I can still vividly see the picture of two Americans, and two Filipinos, sitting in the gathering dusk, in an unfinished Church, in that 80-some, grass house village of San Jose, out among the islands, where one water tap serves the entire village, and the four of us talking with simple trust, simply about the need. One Filipino had a 20-foot boat; one American had a vision. But only God has the means, we know. Ah, but that is the way it is meant to be.

"We spent a couple hours more looking over their village, the new boat Tracy was building for his island ministry, sharing, and talking about that small boat ministry. His wife brought us some 'sweet rice.' It was very good.

"As we ate in the shade of that palm thatched roof, Albert said, 'First, of course, they need to know Jesus; but in most fishing Barangays, the critical need is for safe water. We are losing far too many of our children before they can develop a resistance to the organisms that are in most ground water. You saw the children waiting at the one water tap in this village. Some will wait four hours to fill their pails.'

Albert Tracy walking the streets of San Jose.

"'Yes,' Dan continued, 'And we have been teaching them to grow vegetables. They eat so much fish and rice, they are missing crucial vitamins. Many vegetables will grow well here, but the people need to be taught.'

"About 5:00, we waded out to Albert's old boat, about a 20-foot, open, outrigger with a 16 hp Kohler, air-cooled engine. That was some ride back to Surigao just at dark. He let us out right in front of our Hotel.

"This has been a different day, a day I never expected. As I stood there, on that distant shore, and watched that gentle, fine man and his tiny boat blend into the night and the silence, my mind was whirring with ideas for the boats *we* needed for this crucial, crucial work."

Albert Tracy's runabout.

The Boat

At this date, this is the boat it appears we need: A sixty-foot, all-steel catamaran with two decks, plus a wheelhouse. The catamaran for several reasons: It could rest, with stability on the beach over a tide; it is wider, and so will provide more deckspace for its length; the hulls can be much narrower, allowing for much more efficient travel, slicing through the water. (I would hope for ten miles per gallon at ten miles per hour; or better, ten nautical miles per gallon at ten knots.)

Except for the galley and heads (restrooms), the lower deck would be covered, but open to be used for freight or a mobile meeting room. The upper deck to have an office, and six staterooms, plus a spare, for a crew of twelve; that is, Captain and wife, who would double as Administrator and stores clerk; Engineer and wife in charge of all maintenance and cooking; a Medical Doctor and wife/nurse; a horticulturist and wife; a water expert and wife, and an evangelist and wife. All, of course, would assist in cooking, housekeeping and other chores.

There should be a ramp and small deck space forward for a small jeep and/or motorbikes, and a space on the stern for a tent in folded package. A hoist should be there for off-loading the tent. The ship should carry two shore boats, one, perhaps, a small hovercraft for reaching beaches too shallow even for a small boat.

And with a minimum of 60 feet, the ship would be seaworthy enough to run to or from the Philippines in about 24 days every six months. Pastor Pacleb tells us that the work can be effectively done, only during the six months of dry season. Going over, the ship can carry Bibles, clothing, and other special needs. At home the crew would receive the needed R & R, and the ship could receive drydocking, painting and repair.

In Place

Well, what do we have in place now for this ambitious project?

In the Philippines, we have Albert Tracy with his needed blend of American and Filipino heritage, and with his knowledge of the waters and weather and tides. In Dumaguete, we have Pastor Benito Pacleb, and his 80-some Church Organization, the Full Gospel Fellowship of Churches and Ministers of the Philippines. They can supply Evangelists, Bible School Students on on-the-job training, fuel, food, and liaison with local authorities.

We have organizations such as YWAM, who, said Dan Heinzman, could use such a platform as this boat to send in horticulturists to teach the people about growing those needed vegetables. We have the 700 Club's Operation Blessing, who should welcome such a platform, a tiny, floating, but very real island of America, from which to send forth a medical team. We have such organizations as "Life

Water International," who should equally grasp the opportunity to send forth water experts on this ship.

And, we have a shipyard, who can build these boats at the highest quality, lowest cost ratio of any in the business. [Much prayer, and some readjustments, stopped the flow of red ink of that one year. They are in the black again.] Yes, of course they would have to make at least a nominal profit; they have a hundred families depending on their fiscal success. Still, after a few boats, all identical, that cost can be greatly reduced even though the quality and thus the safety of the crew would remain. And, because this is a very real, Christian outfit, their integrity is beyond reproach. Although I have not at all discussed audit with them, I know that their books on any of these boat projects would be open to audit by any auditor sent by a qualified organization, such as the Full Gospel Fellowship of Churches.

The Heart Of God

I realize now, as I complete this story, that Capt. Dean Nichols, himself, may never run a boat in the Philippines. But if just one (better 100, of course) but if just one of the seeds I am scattering now falls on fertile ground, we will see that this message is truly from the heart of God.

Please pray that the Lord of the harvest will send a hundred boats, to carry the laborers with the skills and knowledge of good water, good food, and good health, but mostly with the knowledge of the Good News of Jesus, to the 58 million people on the 7000 islands of the Philippines.

Please pray with me.

> Capt. Dean Nichols
> Umpqua Valley Christian Fellowship
> Wilbur, Oregon
> U.S.A.

www.ingramcontent.com/pod-product-compliance
Lightning Source LLC
Chambersburg PA
CBHW050350230426
43663CB00010B/2060